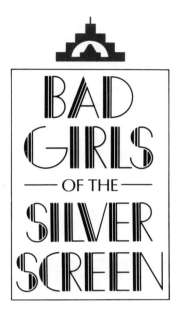

BAD GIRLS OF THE SILVER SCREEN

LOTTIE DA

JAN ALEXANDER

PANDORA

LONDON • SYDNEY • WELLINGTON

First published in Great Britain by Pandora Press, an imprint of the Trade Division of
Unwin Hyman Limited, in 1990.
Designed and Produced by Peter Elek Associates, 457 Broome Street, New York, NY 10013

Pandora Press
Unwin Hyman Limited
15-17 Broadwick Street
London W1V 1FP

Allen & Unwin Australia Pty Ltd
8 Napier Street, North Sydney, NSW 2060, Australia

Allen & Unwin New Zealand Pty Ltd with the Port Nicholson Press
Compusales Building, 75 Ghuznee Street, Wellington, New Zealand

British Library Cataloguing in Publication Data

A CIP catalogue record for this book is available on request from The British Library.

ISBN 0-04-440601-0

Printed in Canada

For our Mothers, and for Mae West, the High Priestess of screen sexuality.

CONTENTS

ACKNOWLEDGEMENTS

Many individuals, private collectors, institutions, archives, and corporations have warmly and willingly assisted the authors in seeking out and providing information and stills in the compilation of this volume. We have tried to attribute ownership in material contained herein correctly, but if inadvertently we have erred, we apologize and will be happy to attempt correction in any subsequent reprinting, if so advised. The authors thank the following:

Priscilla Alexander
Mark, Margaret, Romir Baptista
Bertha Baskin
Willie Bishop
Lizzie Borden
British Film Institute
Jack Broadley
Gary Brown
Italia and Alida Calabro
William Claxton
Brien Coleman
Columbia Pictures
Norma Connoly
Suzan Cooper
Mary Corliss
Bob Cosenza
Jeremy Cox
Father de Paul Genska and the
  Catholic Theology Seminary
Uncle Dick
Larry Draper
Ward Dunham
George Eastman House
Anne Edelstein
George Eels
Mary Emmerick
Lois Erikson
Eva
Taylor Evans
William K. Everson
Murray Farr
Henry Fera
David and Deeane Fetcheimer
Sheila Finn
First National Pictures
Leslie Fishbein
Joe Franklin
Dolores French
David Frazier and the

Kinsey Institute
Terry Geesken
Jeff Goldberg
Maureen Goldsmith
Garry Goodrow
Jane & Howard Grad
Herb Graff
Rose Gramaglia
David Grossman
Dino Harrington
Will Hays, Jr.
Delilah Jackson
De Metrie Kabbaz
Tamar Karet
Ray Katz
Kimo
Lindy King
Mark Koo
Jane Lahr
Richard Lamparski
Lois Lee
Betty Lewis
The Staff of Lincoln Center
  Library/Theatre &
  Film Collection
Gloria Lockett
Patrick Loughney
Ian Loveseth
Wynn Loving
Lucas Films
Tom Luddy
John Lyons
Ed Maguire
Malvinas Cafe
Howard Mandelbaum
Ron Mandelbaum
Mary-Lynn Matvey
Sandy McKenzie
Giles Mead

Vaughan Meader
Metro Pictures
Bleusette Meyers
Deborah Meyers
MGM
Eric Miller
Mario, Habiiba, Raoul,
  Maoshe Miranda
Dr. Michael Moles
Monique Montgomery
Carol Morro
Dennis Murray and
  West Beach Cafe
NOW
Lola & Ayan Owens
Pacific Film Archives
Paramount
Jo-Anne Parrent
Betsey Perry
Gail Pheterson
Photofest
Oliver Rish
RKO
Malcolm Ross III
Maria-Rosa Sclauzero
Sam Segal
Charles Silver & Ron &
  the staff at the MOMA
  Film Study Center
Anthony Slide
Jonathon Slon
Scott Smith
David Sperry
Margo St. James
Gene Stavis
Kay Steeves
Jay Stover
Mr. and Mrs. Neal Tellis
Turner Network

20th Century-Fox
United
United Artists
Marvin Usevich
Ann Wehr
Ralph Wells
Mindy Werner
Sandi-Rose West
Anthony Williams
Patsy Wong
Michael Zivian
Al Zuckerman

And a special thanks to
Kris Di Lorenzo,
our matchmaker.

Peter Elek Associates gratefully acknowledges the dedication of the
following in the production of this volume:

Carolyn Brunton
Brian Collins
Jeffrey Fackler
Kathy Flemming
Robert Hamilton
Robert Hillegas
Liza Lagunoff
Sue Llewellyn
Martha N. Solonche
and especially, Helene Winkler-Elek

In researching *Bad Girls of the Silver Screen*, we viewed about 800 American films and catalogued over 2000, some of which no longer exist, dating from the early 1900s to the present. Although we also saw many foreign films, we decided to focus on the movies that best represented American society's attitudes toward women and sex in each era; hence this became a book almost exclusively devoted to Hollywood films. We realize that many beloved movies and actresses are not discussed in this book; this is because there are so many movies about "scarlet" women and we simply did not have the space to give them the attention and esteem that they deserve.

PREFACE

When we were young movie mavens in the 1950s and 1960s, we often wistfully imagined growing up to be the glamorous women on the Hollywood screen—the ones with the long crimson fingernails and low-cut evening gowns. Even veiled references to a "shameful" life seemed rather enticing to our impressionable young minds. Yet unlike the sizzling swashbuckling male renegade who usually ended up conquering civilizations or ruling nations, the female counterpart would always end up suffering—or darning socks for a man willing to forgive her "mysterious past."

"Easy virtue" and prostitution have been mainstays of the movies since the invention of the motion picture camera. Although we knew on-screen Hollywood had long adhered to a production code that mandated either reform, punishment, or death for the woman who performs sexual favors in return for money, material goods, or career advancement, the question remained—did these portrayals reflect or affect off-screen Hollywood and American society in general?

Throughout the broad history of film, the portrayal of "bad girls" has remained much the same. The packaging has varied with the decade, and the presentation has become more subtle. Early films served as creator and innovator. Over the years, films have become more complex, both creating and reflecting Hollywood's ever-changing view of the world. The nature of Hollywood has evolved.

THE FALL FROM INNOCENCE AND THE WHITE SLAVE

One little girl, fair as a pearl
Worked every day in a laundry;
All that she made for food she paid
So she slept on a park bench so soundly;
An old procuress spied her there,
She came and whispered in her ear:

Chorus:
Come with me now, my girly,
Don't sleep out in the cold,
Your face and tresses curly
Will bring you fame and gold,
Automobiles to ride in, diamonds
and silk to wear;
You'll be a star bright, down in the red light,
You'll make your fortune there.

Same little girl, no more a pearl,
Walks all along 'long the river;
Five years have flown, her health is gone,
She would look at the water and shiver;
Whene'er she'd stop to rest and sleep
She'd hear a voice call from the deep:
(Chorus)

Girls in this way fall every day,
And have been falling for ages,
Who is to blame? You know his name,
It's that boss that pays starvation wages.
A homeless girl can always hear
Temptation calling everywhere:*
(Chorus)

....

"Fifty girls in chains! See the white slave trade bigger than life!" the ads announced, while honky tonk pianos played in the background. The lights were bright in the tenement back alleys. There was a carnival every night when the dry goods stores cleared away their day business and turned into miniature vaudeville palaces. On the screen, *The Fatal Hour* was beginning. The beautiful heroine writhed in terror, tied to a bed in a deserted shack. Pong Lee, occupation white slave panderer, had another young innocent for sale. As the clock ticked away toward 12 noon, the fatal hour, the damsel prepared to meet her doom. Enter the hero, just in time.

No one in the audience knew who the

---

*"The White Slave" by Joe Hill; from Songs of the Workers to Fan the Flames of Discontent, 1913 edition; reprinted by Industrial Workers of America, 1973.

1

leading lady was. It was 1908, and Biograph paid her well—about $10 a day—but all the studios kept their players anonymous. Just as well, for the actors. It was an easy buck while this nickel picture show fad lasted, but a young woman wouldn't want her mother to know she was making a living that way.

To the $6-week factory girls who couldn't afford three meals a day, any offer of money would be hard to resist. To escape their bleak lives they went to the pictures almost every night. Many were recent arrivals in America, but you didn't need to understand English to brave the adventures of cops and robbers, pirates, cowboys, painted ladies and captive white slaves. And the price was right.

On a girl's way out, some slimy swain might approach her. "A drink?" he might offer. "The pleasure of walking you home? How'd you like to be on the stage? How'd you like to be in the pictures? Or make money any way you can?"

Once in a great while, scouts did look around New York and Chicago for pretty faces attached to shabby dresses, because girls who needed the money badly enough might be willing to work as movie extras. But more likely, a man who hung around the picture shows was looking for candidates for the world's oldest profession.

On the teeming urban streets almost any young woman could make $50 to $400 a week. Some factory girls stood on corners whenever they needed money for a new pair of shoes. The demand for prostitutes was immense in the cities, and the supply of women who saw this as an acceptable alternative or supplement to less-well-paying jobs was almost adequate, but not quite. Hence, white slave traffic was booming.

Pimps and procurers, known as cadets, combed the slums, and even went out into the sticks when they needed more brothel workers. They promised impoverished girls jobs as maids, governesses, actresses, or singers. Some cadets even promised themselves as husbands. Then they'd give the girl spiked wine, take her to the red light district, rape her, take her clothes, and put her to work. Frequent beatings and the heavy debts incurred for purchasing the harlot regalia, along with the knowledge that she was too tarnished to go home, usually kept the white slave from escaping.

This was one more reason that ladies' clubs and ministers wanted to put a stop to nickel shows. "There are always a lot of girls hanging around the nickel theatres who are stage struck, and it's dead easy to get them," one convicted white slaver admitted to the police.

The tabloid headline writers knew that a scandal was as good as a war when it came to increasing circulation. "Fifty Thousand Girls Disappeared This Year" guaranteed a great day for sales. Everyone was worried about protecting young girls from vice, the pulpit word for prostitution. Edison's Kinetoscope, and with it the amazing new moving picture, arrived in the United States at the same time as a massive purity movement. Vice was the source of debate among every imaginable faction.

"In entering the business world the seclusion of the home is lost, and girls become more masculine in their ideas and

Traffic In Souls
It all began when Jack Cohn got the brainstorm to produce a feature film, *Traffic in Souls*. He said, "When *Traffic in Souls* opened, crowds broke the doors to get in. It grossed more than $450,000." The leading lady, Jane Gail, tried to convince Cohn to give the picture a "less lurid title." The profits gave Harry and Jack Cohn enough money to start Columbia Pictures.

OPPOSITE: *Thoroughly Modern Millie*
Beatrice Lillie as Mrs. Meers, the concierge of the Priscilla Hotel for Single Young Ladies, is shown here injecting an apple with a drug. Then she ships the girls away to May's Tart Shop in Peking. Of the movie Lillie said, "The only trouble with this picture is that I don't sing."

ABOVE: *The Devil's Needle*
By now audiences had developed a taste for "sensational" stories due to the white slave films. Drugs were now added in the first sophisticated film on this subject. In this tale, released in 1916, an artist's model becomes a dope addict and is forced to marry a much older man. A charming, love-thwarted model hooks her ex-lover, Tully Marshall, seen here marrying another woman (Margarite Marsh), on drugs. This picture was so popular that it was re-made in 1923.

modes of life. By the establishment of the minimum wage the salaries of men will ultimately be increased. This...will enable young men to marry and thus, to a great degree, at least, make it unnecessary for women to seek employment. This to my mind is the solution to the entire problem," said Illinois Lieutenant Governor Barratt O'Hara, who investigated the relationship between sin and "that boss that pays starvation wages."

"Vice is a frame of mind," insisted a merchant named William C. Thorne, who had worked out a budget showing that any girl adrift in Chicago could keep her expenses down to $8 a week.

"Prostitution will disappear as soon as

women get the vote," proclaimed Jane Addams, the social reformer who founded Hull House.

On Broadway, *The Lure* was the most popular play in town. It told of a young girl snared while buying medicine for her sick mother. But "Madam" had her side of the story too. "The pious landlords who preach against us and charge us twice the rent" were her enemy. *The Lure* and another white slavery play, *The Fight*, both delivered a message that in its time had a socialist bent — that white slavers were in direct alliance with big political machines. The police closed down *The Lure* temporarily due to complaints of "obscenity." When it reopened, the brothel parlor set was gone and an employment office was in its place. Madam's costume was changed from satin and feathers to a prim skirt and blouse.

Eleven city government officials in Chicago thought they might try a similar tactic with the movies. It was 1909, and no one gave much thought to closing down the nickel theatres anymore. It was a tempting idea, but the shows were just too popular. The eleven-man board, however, was concerned that the rubes seemed to believe anything they saw on the bigger-than-life screen. Years before, people had fainted as Louis Lumiere's chugging train rolled head-on toward the audience. And they cheered for the characters who seemed most real — even the bad guys. The customers for the early hand-cranked picture shows had loved *The Way They Do Things on the Bowery*, which featured a harridan who spiked an unsuspecting farmer's drink, plundered his pockets, and had him arrested.

The Chicago men became the country's first film censorship committee that same year. Their first mission was to see that insinuations of rape at the hands of a white slaver weren't there just for the thrill of it all. Vice and sin, the committee dictated, must not be rewarded.

About that time a Chicago police inspector conceded that the new moving picture industry wasn't all bad: "Nickel theatres have done more to injure the saloon business in Chicago than any other factor."

Moviemakers took a cue from the inspector. With other cities establishing censorship boards, the moviemakers had to find a way to clean up their act. Perhaps they could become a voice for the moral fabric of America after all and expose their greatest rival for customers at the same time. And so the temperance drama became the hottest picture of 1909. One short frame showing a groveling, trembling drunkard was all it took to demolish business at the saloon next door. One glass of beer could lead to dt's and death, according to the picture screen.

For a while everything felonious happened in a saloon. As Katusha in a 1909 version of Tolstoy's *Resurrection*, Florence Lawrence, known then as simply "the Biograph girl." beat an almost instantaneous path from the arms of her seducer to a saloon. There she peddled her charms and soon found herself arrested for a murder she didn't commit. The Bible showed Katusha the error of her ways and she refused the temptation of a government pardon, instead marching off through the Siberian snow, gazing rapturously skyward. A review in *Motion*

Picture World said, *"Resurrection* is of course a moral lesson ....We think it really wonderful that the Biograph Company should handle this theme with such fidelity and consciousness." The fidelity, clearly, was not to the original novel, but to some higher calling.

Morality made the movies grow. Upright citizens from the better side of town didn't mind seeing moral lessons. They didn't mind paying quarters instead of nickels, either, and for the 50- to 90-minute epics *Quo Vadis*, *Queen Elizabeth*, and *Cabiria*, imported from Europe, a dollar wasn't too much to ask. So far American filmmakers had concentrated on 20-minute shorts, but longer features seemed to be the wave of the future.

D.W. Griffith, with his stable of angelic young girls, was, like everyone else in 1913, churning out one- and two-reelers.

Innocence turned the master on and old-fashioned Southern womanhood was a part of his inspiration for an epic multi-reeler. However, he was not to be the first American to come out with a financially successful full-length feature film. At Universal Studios, a lesser known director named George Loane Tucker got excited when he saw a staid document entitled "Commercialized Prostitution in New York City." He wanted

OPPOSITE: *The Penalty*
Claire Adams begs for mercy. The advertisments read: "The face of satan, the brain of a genius, the body of a monster, the strength of a master of men."

BELOW: *Sal of Singapore*
A dance-hall girl finds maternal instincts rising in her after being shanghaied to look after a foundling. Of her film career, Phyllis Haver noted, "If there was ever a bad woman to be played, I played it, and I'm the kind that believes domesticity is the one career for a woman."

to make a big movie, and this hefty vice commission report by John D. Rockefeller's Bureau of Social Hygiene gave him an idea for a film that would be long, thrilling, racy, lucrative, and socially concerned, like *The Lure* and *The Fight*. He might even be able to call it educational, with the proper plug from Rockefeller. He'd do the old familiar square-up number, with the white slave traders carted off to jail and the damsel rescued with her virtue intact.

Tucker confided his idea to Jack Cohn, an editor at the studio.

"Let's do it!" exclaimed the ecstatic Cohn. His father had been a policeman who worked near the Tenderloin station in New York, and as a boy Jack had been allowed to sit atop the carriage when the cops raided the houses of ill repute. It was one of his most thrilling childhood memories.

The two of them rushed to tell Carl Laemmle, the president of Universal. They thought he'd go for the idea, even though "Uncle Carl" believed in "wolume." He had made his fortune cranking out two-reelers faster than anyone else, but he also had a passion for trying out new film techniques. Once, he had brought over a German inventor to work on hand-coloring film, and then he had found another German who had devised a clumsy machine that synchronized sound with pictures. In both cases, Laemmle had become tired of putting out the money

The Devil Dancer
The "girl with ball-bearing hips" is kidnapped by a slave owner and then rescued. If the Gilda Gray fans of the shimmy still have a desire to see her shake it up, what she does in *The Devil Dancer* is worth the price of admission. When the film went on tour, Sam Goldwyn arranged for Gilda Gray to be there and dance for the audience. The tickets were $3 and Gray "did voodoo and oriental dances." Gray was a protégée of Sophie Tucker and the originator of the shimmy.

before his protégés were able to perfect their gadgets. He'd also created the first movie star in 1910, when he enticed Florence Lawrence away from Biograph, signed her to an exclusive contract, and got her name in the papers by staging her "premature death."

This time, Laemmle's first question was, "How much will it cost?"

"Five thousand," Tucker replied.

"Remember, we give 'em wolume," Uncle Carl thundered. "NO. No, no, no." For $5,000 he could make eleven or twelve short films.

Tucker and Cohn left the boss's office disappointed but not defeated.

"We'll do it anyway," Tucker resolved.

They told three other Universal employees, Herbert Brenon, King Baggot, and Bob Daly, about Tucker's brainstorm, and all agreed it was a most worthy investment. They would finance and produce the film themselves. Luck was with them, because Laemmle was preoccupied with the patent war — perhaps that was why he canned the idea in the first place. (He was one of the independents, not licensed by the Motion Picture Patents Company, also known as the "Trust.") Laemmle and the other independent producers — William Fox, Adolph Zukor, Jesse Lasky and Samuel Goldfish among them — were still trying to put up a legal fight to stop the Trust goons from breaking their cameras, as they did periodically. Eventually the independents, most of them Jewish immigrants who had fled their homeland as boys and come to the New

World to seek their fortunes in garments and dry goods before pictures came along, would have to flee civilization entirely, and set up motion picture camps in southern California.

Tucker, a former stage actor himself, found two somewhat experienced actresses, Jane Gail and Ethel Grandin, to star in his movie—with billing—and plenty of others happy to work without having their names revealed. During lunch breaks, after the daily wraps, any time there was a lull in regular production, Tucker and his cohorts gathered the cast and shot the story. They ended up with ten reels, which Cohn cut to six.

Gail and Grandin played two sisters who worked in a candy store. Tucker gave them an invalid inventor father who wore a yarmulke (skullcap) and tinkered all day with electrical sound devices; he thought Laemmle would like that. The plan, after all, was to please the head honchos and talk them into buying the film back.

At last the film was completed, to the tune of $5,700, and ready for exhibition. Tucker went to Uncle Carl, confessed what he'd done, and begged for a chance to screen the evidence. Laemmle and the board of directors watched the suspenseful story of the little sister's capture and release ... and finally, to Tucker's great relief, agreed to pay for it.

The first American feature film to make a hit, *Traffic in Souls*, opened in New York in 1913, four months before Griffith's *Judith of Bethulia* opened and more than a year before audiences saw *Birth of a Nation*. Thirty thousand people dutifully paid their quarters to see *Traffic in Souls* the first week it ran. All told, the picture made $450,000, even without playing the second largest market—Chicago had banned it. The Board of Censors felt their sin detectors go off when they saw the ad:

The Half Way Girl
Doris Kenyon portrays Poppy La Rue, a chorus girl stranded in Shanghai and forced to Malay Street. One of the titles in the movie read, "I'm not a bad girl, not a good girl, just a half way girl; half good impulses, half bad impulses."

"The sensational motion picture dramatization based on the Rockefeller White Slavery Report and the investigations of the Vice Trust by District Attorney Whitman. A $200,000 spectacle in 700 scenes with 800 players showing the traps cunningly laid for young girls by vice agents. Don't miss the most thrilling scene ever staged — the smashing of the Vice Trust."

This was something less than truth in advertising, but interestingly enough, Tucker did make an attempt to expose the greed and corruption at the top that kept the white slave traffic alive. Much of the plot revolves around William Trubus, a prominent pillar of the community. While the candy store girls Mary (Gail) and Lorna (Grandin) arise early every morning to support themselves and their ailing father, Trubus's daughter lounges around in her nightgown all day. As the movie begins, Trubus has just been elected head of the International Purity and Reform League, but it's just a cover. After he nods a good morning to his gum-cracking secretary, he goes into his private office and puts on a set of headphones which look just like a Walkman headset—but the music Trubus hears is the sound of money changing hands down the hall, in an office where the white slave cadets make all of their deposits.

Each day, the "vice agents" haunt the train stations and the docks. One morning they find a couple of robust country lasses fresh off the train, promise them jobs, and take them to a brownstone house where a swarthy madam awaits the new arrivals, cracking her whip whenever the inmates annoy her. The country girls are tough enough to fight their way out, but two Swedish sisters with long blonde braids aren't so lucky. Although their brother is there to meet them when their boat arrives, the waiting cadets use one of their

many ruses. One cadet walks up to the brother and begins to insult him. Finally, the brother punches him and is promptly arrested. The second snake, posing as a sympathetic bystander, announces, "I will take your sisters home." He takes them to the brownstone, where there's now a sign in the window that says "Swedish Employment Agency."

Meanwhile, little sister Lorna has fallen for a charming fellow who keeps hanging around the candy store. She makes a date with him, over her sister's protests. He plies her with fine food and wine and takes her dancing. The night has grown late by the time the knockout drug he slipped into her wine begins to take effect. She wakes up in a strange room and realizes right away that the one Fate Worse Than Death awaits her.

Mary loses her job "on account of her sister's disgrace." But it just so happens that Mrs. Trubus has caught her husband's secretary kissing a cadet on the job, so the missus throws out the old secretary and installs Mary, her favorite candy store clerk, in the post. From there, it's easy for Mary to discover the headset, listen in, and recognize the voice of the fiend who captured her sister. As the prisoner bravely resists her captors, refusing to eat and refusing to package herself in a flimsy black negligee, Mary and her fiancé, Police Officer Burke, are setting up the original Watergate bugging system in Trubus's office. They get all the evidence they need to stage a knock-'em-out raid scene. Mr. and Mrs. Trubus die of shame, and Little Sister is saved in the Nick of Time.

Just three weeks after *Traffic in Souls* opened, *The Inside of the White Slave Traffic* came out and cashed in on a sure thing. The Sociological Research Film Corporation could brag that this was a sort of documentary, since they showed real feminine traders in pulchritude, and even some real customers. A former government investigator had even supervised the production. They stretched the pedigree in the ad, however:

"This is the only authentic white slave picture ever made having the endorsement of the honorable Henry J. Dannebaun, former assistant attorney general, Justice John L. Sullivan and many others, with the cooperation of the Department of Justice."

In this scenario, the cadet Ed traps the young maiden Virginia with a variation on the concerned bystander trick. His accomplice insults her on the street, then Ed rushes to defend her honor. She thinks she's found her knight in shining armor — until she wakes up in a house of sin. Several hundred people had to be turned away the night *The Inside of the White Slave Traffic* opened in New York.

In the same years that Griffith was producing his spectacles, Mack Sennett his illustrious slapstick, and William Fox's vampire woman was wrecking every man in sight, white slavery movies also made big bucks. A poetic string of titles claimed to educate audiences: *The Lure of New York, The Shame of the Empire State, The Thorns of the Great White Way, The Great Lure of Paris, Human Cargoes, Daughters of Despair, The Dupe, Evil Hands, Protect Your Daughter, Smashing the Vice Trust, The Serpent of the Slums.*

Yet when *Traffic in Souls* "educated" the public by revealing what the inside of a brothel looked like, it was shockingly risqué. The editors of *Motion Picture World* and *Variety* agreed that the white slave pictures were "injurious to the public health," and both papers refused to advertise or review them after February 1914.

Soon the hottest issue of the 1910s became a moot point, however, because shortly after America entered the Great War in 1916, people seemed to forget about white slavery as more modern concerns took hold. When the police shut down New Orleans's legendary Storyville the next year, the purity crusaders thought they had won the war against red light districts. Indeed they had demolished the ghettoes, but prostitutes and pimps simply moved into new neighborhoods and learned to operate with more secrecy. What was left of the purity movement turned its sights to birth control, and Universal obligingly made *Where Are My Children?*, a movie that proved that only selfish, immoral women practiced the art of non-conception.

The white slavery movie itself became passé as the country's Victorian hangover, and with it, the Fate Worse Than Death gambit, began to wear off. By the war's end, a man named Sigmund Freud had explained to the Western world that women did have a sex drive after all. Modern girls called themselves flappers. They didn't care much about old-fashioned morality, and many of them dreamed not of marriage and respectability, but of running off to join the movie gypsies who were setting up shacks amid California's orange groves, in a dusty hamlet called Hollywood. Out there, the only sin was obscurity.

VAMPS
AND COURTESANS

A fool there was and he made his prayer
(Even as you and I!)
To a rag and a bone and a hank of hair
(We called her the woman who did not care).
But the fool he called her his lady fair
(Even as you and I!)*

. . . .

W hen Theodosia Goodman—Teddy to her friends—was 18, she left her home in Cincinnati with high hopes of acting on Broadway. Her father, a Jewish tailor, gave her a little money even while pleading with her to change her mind. But Teddy was determined. All the perky ingenue with the baby-fat cheeks and big dark eyes could get that first year, 1909, was a $25-a-week bit part with a road company—but at least the white slavers didn't get her.

The show led to nothing. A few years passed, and Theodosia got used to being hungry. When a man stopped her in the street and timidly told her, "I'm an agent for the motion pictures ... you'd photograph well. I could get you a job for $175 a week," she told him that she wouldn't think of it. Not even for a million dollars.

She wasn't desperate enough to sell out to the pictures until her apartment caught fire. Finally, 23-year-old Theodosia went to call on Frank Powell, an acquaintance who was directing a picture called *The Stain* for Fox Studios.

"Do you think you could give me a part?" she asked. Having lost most of her possessions in the fire, she was able to muster a little genuine enthusiasm.

Powell looked her over. His imagination started working overtime. He liked the impression of her dark, sad eyes against her malnourished pallor. There was a searching look in those eyes that could be very erotic, he decided. Actually, she was only searching for a focus on his face—Theodosia was very

---

Dr. Jekyll and Mr. Hyde
Nita Naldi (shown here with John Barrymore) lamented that "I am always cast for the vampire parts, when I would like so much to play a nice sweet little girl. You don't think I can play ingenues...but if they want a wild wicked woman to ruin a man's reputation and extort all his money from him, they think I'm fine."

---

*First verse of "The Vampire" by Rudyard Kipling, 1897.

near-sighted.

William Fox applauded Powell's new find and called in his two best press agents, Johnny Goldfarp and Al Selig, who, from a starving, astigmatic ingenue, fashioned the screen's first sex symbol. They christened her Theda Bara.

Theodosia found herself with a brand new name, a new image, and a new hometown. Theda Bara—unscrambled, that spelled "Arab Death"—had been born beneath the Sphinx. Her father was a French artist who had lost

his senses in the mystic embrace of an Arab princess. Their offspring was the kind of woman who would relish drinking a man's blood for breakfast. She was the Vampire Woman —the Kipling poem image in the flesh.

A Fool There Was, released in 1915, introduced the Vampire Woman with a huge white rose at her heaving breasts, dragging along a withered little victim, a fool so shaky

he can't light the cigarette that dangles limply from his lips. He cannot help but follow her to the ship *Gigantic*, on which she plans to stalk her next prey, and shoots himself.

As the Vampire undulates up the gangplank, respectable wives shield their husbands' eyes. But John Schuyler (Edward José), a government envoy on an official trip to England, has no protection from her hungry gaze. Months later, they're on the Italian Riviera together. He's already a little weaker, sitting beside her chaise lounge, his tie loosened, sipping wine from a tiny goblet. The Vampire stretches languidly in a catlike pose that says she's satiated for the moment.

With each subsequent scene, John looks a little older and a little feebler. The Vampire won't let him see his faithful wife, his friends disown him and the servants walk out. Soon his hair has turned white, and his eyes bulge from his shriveled face. His once-elegant townhouse resembles the city dump. He never appears without a whiskey bottle in his grasp.

At last John the Fool, who can no longer stand upright, breaks his neck while crawling down the staircase. The Vampire, with a satisfied smirk on her face, strews rose petals over the corpse.

Without a break between movies, Bara went on to play a Russian adulteress, a wicked wife whose husband slays her, the devil's daughter, and an Italian peasant siren. Before the year 1915 was up, Fox's scenario writers had cooked up her first classic role. She was to play Carmen, the great bitch goddess of literary and operatic fame, in a picture that Raoul Walsh would direct.

Legend had it that Prosper Mérimée wrote the novella *Carmen* 15 years after a raven-haired waitress served him "the devil's gazpacho." His Carmen was a gypsy. Under

OPPOSITE: *Carmen*
Before shooting this version starring Theda Bara, all the men shaved their heads for good luck. William Fox hired real gypsies who were a source of constant wonder as the men were so strong and the women sold Spanish medicine, told fortunes, and begged.

ABOVE: *Carmen*
Jeanie Macpherson fought really hard but she was merely trying to keep her wig on. De Mille produced this version with the opera star Geraldine Farrar. The bull scenes were directed by Spanish toreadors and the bulls were brought in from Mexico. When Geraldine Farrar returned to the role at the Met, she continued to fight hard, stating, "Mr. De Mille understood my enthusiasm and left me free to express natural impulses."

LEFT: *Vamp*
The young man lies there in an excited state, and the seductress, turned into a real vampire, devours him. Star Grace Jones proclaimed, "I'm the first narcissist vampire. My blood was black and chocolatey, his blood was sweetened with something. It was sort of icky yucky, but it tasted good. I bruised him by accident but he loved every minute of it." The vamp-to-vampire part was originally offered to Tina Turner.

19

her hex, the brave soldier Don Jose withered away into a state of drooling delirium, finally stabbing her in a fit of jealous rage.

"I have felt a strange sensation whenever I have thought of this girl, Carmen, of the Spanish hills. The mere thought of her gives me a thrill. There is now plenty of evidence that Mérimée wrote down almost the exact life of the girl Ar Minz, whom he met in Spain..... It seems to me that I know all these events... that I was Carmen herself," Bara told a gathering of reporters. Her past life regression was another Goldfarp and Selig creation. The maid interrupted this press conference to bring in Bara's vampire lunch of raw beef and lettuce.

Thanks to the Fox publicity mill, Theda Bara, whether she was the reincarnation of Carmen or not, possessed the secret shared by all legendary she-devils. Louis XV lost his senses when Madame Du Barry dazzled him. Thanks to her, the king hardly noticed that the populace was brewing a revolution. Camille, the silver screen's second most beloved minx after Carmen (judging by the number of film versions made in this century), was just a wistful fantasy on the part of Alexandre Dumas fils. Dumas was smitten by a Parisian courtesan who toyed with his affections and told him, "Lying keeps my teeth white." When the real Camille, a swan-necked beauty named Marie Duplessis, died of consumption, Dumas imagined her with a nobler heart than all those who condemned her. The novel he wrote won him a place in the charmed circle of Left Bank bohemia, but he never won her love. And Theda Bara? A lover once killed himself with her poison snake bracelet, according to the fan magazines.

Carmen, Camille, and all of the world's great seductresses were deft in the art of draining a man's purse, of course. But that wasn't their diabolical secret. Far more important was to rob each fool of a far more priceless and irreplaceable resource—his great sperm count!

The vampire that Bara played was really a ninteenth century character that thrived on the silver screen for a brief period before the Modern Age took hold in the 1920s and the nation conceded that gender roles were not entirely separate and unequal. The Vampire's power came from the old scientific "fact" that loss of sperm made men weak. If a man wasted his precious fluid in nonprocreational emissions, scientists believed he'd develop dementia, infectious diseases, and/or neurological disintegration. Mercifully, wrote Dr. William Acton in the 1870s, God created woman to be indifferent to sex, thus saving man from his own lust.

But not the Vampire. She craved man's vital juices. When Bara played Carmen she was Rubenesque; as Camille and Du Barry she was plumper still. In her later movies, *Cleopatra* and *Salome*, she was downright hefty by today's standards—as though she were consuming fools by the hundreds.

Though Bara laid claim to the soul of Carmen, this was the first movie to bring her competition as the reigning Vampire. Out in Hollywood, Cecil B. De Mille, casting his own Carmen for Lasky Studios, would have none other than the très elegant prima donna Geraldine Farrar.

"But I must have a private car on the train," Farrar insisted before she agreed to make the trek out west. That was easily arranged.

Farrar was thrilled when she met her Don Jose—handsome, wholesome "Good Time Wally" Reid. They got rave reviews together, but Bara's *Carmen* was a box office hit too.

Camille
It is said that Sarah Bernhardt fainted when she saw herself on
the screen in this 1912 version. She hated filmmaking and had
to be harrassed by creditors before showing herself in "these
absurd photographic pantomimes."

ABOVE: *Camille*
Clara Kimball Young commented to the screenwriter Frances
Marion: "Oh shit, it's another of these stories, it's the fault of
old smellsick [Selznick] all I've got to do is cough, kiss a
Frenchie named Armand and die. When my contract ends, I'll
drink champagne, smoke cigarettes, and spit in the public's
eye."

OPPOSITE: *Camille*
Norma Talmadge said of the role: "I like playing Camille if
only because of the tradition behind that traditional role and
the sentiment that is so much a part of it, but a star has a big
responsibility on her shoulders as she influences the lives of
thousands of girls...who actually model their future from our
screen conduct."

The next year Charlie Chaplin made yet another version, with his on-again-off-again lady love, Edna Purviance, in the title role.

Meanwhile, Bara, still the only genuine Vampire Woman, kept making a movie a month. And reporters couldn't get enough of the publicity mill concoctions.

"Is this the wickedest face in the world?" began one Sunday feature. Bara read it while breakfasting with her kid sister, Lori, and the two were in stitches all morning. Theda also laughed uproariously over the interview with Nixola Greeley-Smith, in which the Vampire had "confided" the secret of her black art.

"A vampire must never love," she had said, after a careful rehearsal. "I have never loved, and if I ever fall under the spell of man, I know that my power over men will be gone. Every woman must choose whether she will love or be loved. She cannot hope for both. You know we French people have a proverb that in love there is always one who kisses and one who merely turns the cheek. The Vampire is content to turn the cheek. That is why she makes fools of men. But believe me, for every Woman Vampire, there are ten men of the same type, men who take everything from women—love, devotion, beauty, youth—and give nothing in return! V stands for Vampire, and it stands for Vengeance. The Vampire that I play is the vengeance of my sex upon its exploiters. You see, I have the face of a Vampire, perhaps, but the heart of a feministe."

Thanks to the Vampire, teenaged girls were burning incense before male callers arrived. "Baby vamps" powdered their rosy cheeks with chalky camouflage, learned to slither, and adopted the seductive mourning look in a sudden rampant passion for black. But at the same time, children fled when they saw Theda Bara walking down the street.

The feministe Vampire grew nervous when she learned that a woman had strolled into a movie theater, and high-kicked a hole through "the wickedest face in the world" on a poster. "Oh, how I hate you," the woman wrote in a note to Bara, telling her that the

satisfaction of the assault was well worth the $10 fine.

Clearly, Bara needed protection. So the contract she signed in 1917 shielded her from public view and from losing her power. The terms dictated:

1. She was not to marry.
2. She must never appear in public without a heavy veil.
3. She must never ride in a public conveyance.
4. She must never go to a Turkish bath.

When Fox decided to start filming her pictures in California, Bara reluctantly left the apartment she shared with her parents

and sister, who had moved to New York by then and had all changed their names to Bara. Out in the land where the sun shone year-round, movie stars were still living in modest bungalows. They lived for the moment, knowing that tomorrow celluloid might go the way of the horse and buggy. Money was growing like oranges out there, but it went to hooch and joy powder and high living — certainly not to such humdrum investments as real estate. But the Vampire housed in pink stucco? Never, resolved the fortitudinous team of Goldfarp and Selig. They instructed Bara to buy herself something fancy. So she made herself at home in a sprawling mock-Tudor house, festooned inside with tiger skins, crystal balls, skulls, and mummy cases. There the world's wickedest woman spent her leisure hours distilling perfume and gazing into the astrological charts, or so the tales claimed.

Meanwhile, in Omaha, the Women's Club dedicated their monthly meeting of March 1918 to Theda Bara and her latest display of indecorum, *Cleopatra*, in which she appeared wearing nothing above the waist but jewels and breastplates. Though the ladies declared that the star and the movie were fit for neither children nor adults, *Cleopatra* was a sellout in Omaha, and all across the heartland. Even before the war ended in 1918 and the boys came to home to Theda Bara as

Camille
Darryl Zanuck recalls that Nazimova "was my idea of the quintessential Queen of the Movie Whores, and the nearest Hollywood ever got to showing a star having an orgasm on the screen." "The Woman of a Thousand Moods" once said: "Always I said that I would never play Camille until I had forgotten how I had seen Camille played." After *Camille* she planned to do films with all women — director, writer, actresses. Even Valentino complained about his role: "I am expected to ogle, try to charm and make overtures to every person of the opposite sex without exception."

Salome, decked in pearl drapes and little else, America had become infatuated with anything foreign—even if it was counterfeit foreign. At the war's end, the fruited plains abounded with money, leisure, cars, and dance halls, but the country looked to tinsel-studded Hollywood, and especially Theda Bara's opium-den face, for hints on how to enjoy the new hedonistic commodities. Europeans, like the allegedly half-French Vampire, were said to be sensual, decadent, emotional, sinful, fascinating, dangerous, and potentially evil. Americans felt terminally blah beside them. Any swarthy actress would be typecast as a second-string Bara, while the good girl roles went to flaxen-haired Mary Pickford, who would look quite at home in an Iowa cornfield.

Slowly, genuine exotica began to arrive in Hollywood. Alla Nazimova, a respected star of the stage who made her own film versions of *Salome* and *Camille*, was a slender Russian sylph who made Bara look like a comically vulgar fleshpot. Unbeknownst to American film fans, even Nazimova's sex life was exotic. She was a lesbian, though the fan magazines preferred to tout her happy married existence in the Hollywood home she called the Garden of Allah.

Nita Naldi, an Italian-American, was John Barrymore's temptation in *Dr. Jekyll and Mr. Hyde* of 1920, and a seductress with leprosy, smuggled to America in a bag of Indian jute in De Mille's *The Ten Commandments*. The Polish spitfire Pola Negri looked like Bara with her white face and kohl-rimmed eyes,

but she was younger and trimmer, and demurely vampish in the German import *Passion*, another version of the Madame Du Barry story.

Bara, however, was not particularly worried about the competition. She was getting close to 30 and thinking about her future. What she really wanted was a little versatility. She was fed up with being a seduction machine.

William Fox tried to be gentle but firm. "Your fans love to hate you," he reminded her.

Bara stomped her feet and threw a tantrum worthy of all her past Arab-Gypsy-Latin lives.

"I went on strike and stayed 'struck' until I had my way," she related to *New York Telegram* reporter Jane Dixon. "I refused to vamp another single solitary second unless I was first given the opportunity to prove I could be good just as easily as I was bad. There are no women like that."

There was never a sight more absurd than Bara in corkscrew curls and peasant frock in *Kathleen Mavourneen*. William Fox showed his muscle in the end, and booted her out the door when contract renewal time came.

Though she tried time and again to make a comeback on the stage, fate had an ironic path in store for the Vampire Woman. A director named Charles Brabin captured her heart, and perhaps her powers too. In wedded bliss, Theda Bara became known for her irresistible epicurian repasts—and for having one of the few 'til-death-do-us-part marriages in Hollywood. Birthday cards from Mrs. Brabin to her devoted mate were said to be typically inscribed with such hieroglyphics as "To my darling Mouchy-mou — from your Wiffle Tree."

Pola Negri arrived in New York harbor on a sunny autumn day in 1922. A brass band played for her when she alighted, in her

Madame Du Barry
Star Theda Bara said, "Nobody has ever written a true word about me and it's time the truth was known." Her publicity stated she was from the Nile, but she said: "I was never nearer Egypt than an Egyptian cigarette!"

Cossack dress, high Russian boots, and turban, with twenty seven trunks behind her. America had seen *Passion*, and it was clear who would succeed Bara as queen of the vamps.

Born Appolonia Chalupek she grew up poor in Warsaw, but married a count for a brief spell. Countess Dombski found her castle deadly, so she ran away to the stage in Berlin. There she met Ernst Lubitsch, who put her in films and directed her brilliantly through *Carmen*, *Camille*, and *Madame Du Barry* (retitled *Gypsy Blood*, *The Red Peacock*, and *Passion*, respectively, in the United States). The tempestuous half-gypsy Pola became a star playing seductresses of humble origin.

When Adolph Zukor and Jesse Lasky, the heads of Famous Players/Lasky, saw her flutter her Bara-esque eyelashes at King Louis (Emil Jannings) as he manicured her nails, they knew they had to have her as their own. So she came to America with a generous studio contract.

Negri spent a week in New York rushing from one fete to another. In her rudimentary English, she told the swarm of reporters who followed her, "I think Charlie Chaplin is the most perfect nice moving picture actress is in the screen."

Jesse Lasky gave her a little present as she boarded her train to Hollywood—a book, *Bella Donna*, the inspiration for her first Hollywood role.

She read the story of how Mrs. Chepstowe, who becomes Bella Donna of the Carnival of Venice, steals an Englishman from another woman, vamps him through a honeymoon on the Nile, then falls into the arms of an Arab sheik, and plots with him to murder her husband. A panther in the desert finishes her in the end.

This was not what the new star had had in mind. "I did not feel that my first role in this country should be of another woman devoid of morals or any of the other qualities an audience found sympathetic. It would be terrible if Hollywood thought of me only in terms of playing vamps," she said in her admittedly self-serving memoirs decades later.

But Pola's temperamental style of voicing her protest only fixed the image more firmly. The first day she was to appear on the set, everyone excitedly awaited her arrival. Director George Fitzmaurice and the actors, extras, and crew, waited until 10 a.m., continued waiting until it was nearly noon, and still no sign of the mysterious Miss Negri. At last the phone rang and a voice of undecipherable accent said, "Madame Negri has the misfortune to have a toothache. She will not appear today."

Toothaches, headaches, and conniptions were part of the package, but somehow she managed to complete *Bella Donna*. A smitten critic wrote in *The New York Times*: "No moving picture actress ever filled the role of Kipling's Vampire better than Pola Negri."

So Hollywood happily tolerated her. She claimed she didn't like the warm climate much. Countess Pola found the food in Hollywood bland, and the conversation worse. But if she must be a star in this dusty, decadent town, she would give America fuel for their gossip magazines. So she introduced crimson toenails to American women. Fans looked for her in a block-long white Rolls, trimmed with ivory, with sold gold door handles and white upholstery. A little white pooch always sat in her lap and two white Russian wolfhounds crouched on either side. Her little jazz-boy, Charlie Chaplin, was often seen competing with the pups for her

affections.

Pola and Charlie were engaged. They would coo in the backseat one moment and hurl champagne glasses at each other the next. Charlie was very possessive. His vamp was not to dance with anyone else, and not to smile too broadly at other men. She finally dumped him when he refused to escort her to the premiere of *Bella Donna*—and insisted that she stay home with him instead.

She called a press conference to announce that her engagement was off—this time for good. It was. Other men came along—Rod LaRoque, tennis star Bill Tilden—and finally, true passion entered her life.

"I haf loff!" Pola exclaimed to friends.

Hollywood's perfect match was Pola Negri

Madame Du Barry
"Men could not resist her." Norma Talmadge was known as the Lady of the Great Indoors.

and the great male vamp, Rudolph Valentino.
she was captivated from the moment they
met, when she saw his smoldering, searching
gaze. Like Theda Bara, and like Nita Naldi,
who'd vamped him away from a good woman
in *Blood and Sand*, Rudy had an incredibly
sexy way of straining to see what was in front
of him.

"We were blind as bats," Naldi confessed
to an interviewer years later. "Poor Rudy
groped his way through many a love scene,
and I mean really groped."

But he loved what he could see of Pola.
Ecstasy made her forget her superstitions.
When Pola was very young, she claimed, her
Polish gypsy father foresaw that all the men
she was to love would meet with tragedy.
Indeed, love was to elude Pola, and not just
Valentino's love.

The trouble was, due to circumstances
beyond her control, good and bad girls made
in America were upstaging the vamp. It
started slowly, close to the turn of the
century. Before there were movie moguls
with starlet harems, there was the classically
beautiful Evelyn Nesbit, who at 16 had
already been a chorus girl, an artist's model
for the hoity-toity predecessors of *Penthouse*
photogs, and mistress to prominent New
York architect Stanford White. Her
impoverished childhood had made her
ambitious, and so she became a legendary
homegrown courtesan, the New World
counterpart of Camille. By 18 she had had an
affair with John Barrymore, and married
Pittsburgh millionaire Harry K. Thaw, who
was not only rich, but also crazy, with a
cocaine habit and a taste for S & M. When
Thaw shot White in midst of a celebration at
Madison Square Garden, the whole world
learned of Miss Nesbit's carnal escapades.

While Theda Bara was introducing eros to

OPPOSITE, ABOVE: *The Girl on the Red Velvet Swing*
Joan Collins said: "Anytime there was a tart or a prostitute...I got the part. It was so boring." Discussing the film, Ms. Collins said, "I had to look so perfect and the gorgeous costumes were agony to wear." Evelyn Nesbitt commented, "Don't forget I was only 15 and I enjoyed swinging." Ms. Nesbitt was on the set as a consultant eating cashew nuts to disguise the gin on her breath.

OPPOSITE, BOTTOM: *The Cheat*
The story was filmed three times. With Fanny Ward in 1915, Pola Negri in 1923, and Tallulah Bankhead in 1931. The story

concerns a society wife who gambles and loses $10,000. She borrows it from a playboy and when she pays him back with money, he refuses and brands her! On the set, Fanny Ward was very difficult and had to have paraffin inserted in her cheeks (as she was 40) over and over as it melted from the hot lights. In this version, the villain was played by Sessue Hayakawa, who was also the villain in the 1937 French version, and declared: "It was a pleasure to brand Fanny Ward."

ABOVE: *The Cheat*
Pola Negri was branded by an Indian, and said, "I was again unhappy with the part I was to play...with the exception of the dramatic scene where I was branded."

31

the movie screen, William Randolph Hearst was panting after a doll-faced chorus girl. He fell in love with Marion Davies in 1915 and launched her mostly insipid sugar-and-spice good girl screen career with the help of his media power. "Marion doesn't smoke or drink," Hearst used to say of the pigtailed Peg-o'-his-heart. But there were evenings at Pola Negri's when, rumor had it, Marion would sneak back to the pantry, grab a whole cocktail shaker from the butler, and chug down its contents without wincing. Millicent—Mrs. Hearst—always called Marion "that harlot," all the while following the ancient wifely tradition of tolerating the public humiliation, in exchange for the comforting dictum that wife = saint while mistress = whore.

In 1921, only vamps lolled suggestively on chaise lounges when the cameras were rolling, but Fatty Arbuckle demolished his movie career when he dallied with Virginia Rappe, the Sunbonnet Girl, a wholesome-looking starlet from Chicago, and emerged with a rape and murder rap. He was acquitted but the notoriety ruined him anyway. Not long before that, Olive Thomas, the picture of innocence and wife of Mary Pickford's brother Jack, was found nude, sprawled most unaesthetically on the floor of her Paris hotel suite—very much dead, for unexplained reasons that had to do with her heroin habit. Not long after, good girl Mary Miles Minter and Mack Sennett's favorite clown Mabel Normand both found themselves under arrest. Murder of the very cultured director William Desmond Taylor was the charge. Both of his alleged girlfriends were released, but Mary's career fizzled out and Mabel died a cocaine addict.

Nor were Hollywood's good boys staking any claim to model morality. Negri found

The Cheat
Tallulah Bankhead was branded by an American, Irving Pichel, except the brand was written in Chinese with the expert assistance of Peking University. The brand meant "I Possess." The ad stated, "She gambles at love and is forced to pay a tragic price." Her acting was so bad that she lost her chance to star in *Rain* to Joan Crawford.

that out when she asked for the perfect all-American male as her leading man in *The Cheat*, the story of a diamond-craving young wife who is tempted from the path of virtue. She demanded Wally Reid. When Lasky said no, she pouted and shrieked.

"Very well, Pola, I'll set up an appointment," sighed the studio bigwig. "I think you'll see why we're so against it."

She gasped when the jaundiced, trembling wreck of a man staggered through the door. What Carmen had done to Don Jose, morphine was doing to poor Wally. In January 1923 he died in a padded cell.

Before the band played "Auld Lang Syne" for 1920, the ladies' clubs and Bible-thumpers of America were on the warpath once more. State and city censorship boards were talking about federal legislation to wipe out Hollywood's smell of sin. The motion picture producers realized that their only defense was to regulate their entertainment from within — with morality clauses off-screen, with some upstanding citizen to wield the scissors to any boldly bawdy scene on-screen.

So it was that in December 1921, the wizened, elephant-eared Postmaster General Will Harrison Hays received a round robin letter from Hollywood, offering him a $100,000-a-year salary to leave Washington and come clean up the movies.

The Branding Iron
Branding women was a popular theme in movies of this era. In advertising copy the star Barbara Castleton responds to the question "Do you get any thrills out of movie lovemaking?" "Yes I do. I get a decided thrill out of movie lovemeking; I'm always in love with the man I happen to be playing opposite. While I'm in the man's arms I'm literally in love with him. It may be a matter of intoxication at the moment. It may be mere acting. But whatever the cause, the effect is one of tender passion."

The newly formed Motion Picture Producers and Directors Association had picked Hays because he had launched a crusade against smut in the mails. He appeared to be squeaky clean—a Presbyterian elder, member of the Masons, Rotarians, Knights of Pythias, and the Elks. However, he was content to go down in history as the inventor of airmail. He wasn't enthused about the lucrative offer from show biz, but he promised to think it over during the Christmas holidays while at home in Indiana.

On Christmas morning, his 6-year-old son, Bill, Jr., made up his mind for him. The boy and his cousins were playing cowboys underneath the Christmas tree.

"I'm going to be Bill Hart," a voice declared.

"No, you're not. I am."

"Neither of you is. I am."

Listening to the kids, Hays realized that Bill Hart, the silent screen's most famous cowboy hero, was real to them. He recognized the profound influence that the movies had on millions of children and adults. He decided that it was his Christian duty to accept the position.

Law and order rode into Hollywood the same year that Pola Negri did. Hays claimed that his first concern was for "the mind of a child . . . that unmarked slate," which meant that his favorite scenarios were those geared to the prepubescent view of life. He didn't want little Bill asking, "Daddy, what are that man and woman doing on that chaise lounge?"

Oddly enough, Hays didn't tamper much with the vamp genre, except to encourage Negri and Nazimova to be clothes-horses. One reason he didn't have to change the vamp scripts was that most of the bitch goddesses were suitably punished at the end.

Madame Du Barry died on the guillotine, Carmen at knifepoint, and Camille coughed herself to eternal rest.

Nazimova and Valentino starred in a *Camille* with a boudoir designed for Aphrodite's honeymoon, but Hays never seemed to mind the sight of adults in a bed as long as one of them was sick or wounded. He did, however, nearly keel over when he saw Charlie Chaplin's original version of *A Woman of Paris*, which Chaplin made in 1923. He had gone back to Edna Purviance and cast her as Marie, a courtesan who has to make a tough choice between love and luxury. She chooses the starving artist she loves, but they quarrel and he shoots himself. Chaplin's script had Marie drifting on resignedly as mistress to Pierre Revel (Adolphe Menjou), a gentleman of leisure.

"This condones her immoral lifestyle; she must show remorse," decreed the new czar of virtue. So while European audiences saw the ending as Chaplin meant it to be, Americans saw a homely epistle: "Time heals and experience teaches us that the secret of happiness is service to others," followed by Marie in gingham, happily repentant, running a home for orphans.

But it was not the antiseptic hand of Hays that would bring an end to Pola Negri's idyllic days of stardom, but rather the fun the homegrown Jezebels in Hollywood were having behind the censor's back. The bobbed-hair set was arriving, and fickle audiences were turning their attention to the flapper, who could smoke cigarettes, drink cocktails, flirt, and dance to jazz all night, without losing her apple-pie aura.

The vamp was becoming a relic in the Jazz Age. Paramount (nee Famous Players/Lasky) tried to give Pola the message with *A Woman of the World*, made in 1925. She was playing a countess who flees her unfaithful European lover and visits her cousin in Kansas. There she tries to vamp the local district attorney, who has passed an ordinance against women who smoke. Though she takes a whip to him at the end, and he clearly loves it, the message conveyed in their long final kiss (history has not recorded Hays's reaction to a long string of saliva that the camera picks up as they pull apart) is that he will bring her home to his hearth. "We're taming the tigercat!" ballyhooed the puff agents. They swore that she was rollerskating, eating hot dogs and drinking soda pop on the set, and had even asked to be hit in the face with a cream pie.

Fat chance. Pola had "loff" on her mind. The passionate pas de deux of sheik and vampire was interrupted in the spring of 1926, when Valentino had to go to New York, but he promised he would be back soon. On August 23, however, she received the tragic telegram . . . Rudy would never return. She collapsed, but pulled herself together to walk beside her beloved's casket. Pola wore lavish mourning silks, and cried many overwrought tears as photographers besieged her.

But somewhere, a rumor started that Pola had only been vamping the country's beloved Rudy, and the hysteria was just for the cameras. When she ran off to Paris and married Prince Serge Mdivani less than a year after Valentino's death, her popularity suffered sudden rigor mortis. A nationwide boycott of her new movie, *Barbed Wire*, caused shudders at the box office even though critics acclaimed it.

Pola laid low on the Continent, like an enemy in exile. *Screen Secrets* magazine wiped its nose on the vamp, explaining, "Princess Pola cannot be judged by our standards. Her code is strictly European."

Miss Sadie Thompson
Gloria Swanson was able to produce the film by changing the
title. She even wrote a letter to author Somerset Maugham
asking him to write a sequel! At one point, fifteen studio heads
sent a letter to Joe Schenck, her co-producer, denouncing the
film. Gloria was upset and said, "So why are they sending
telegrams and letters to you....Because I'm a woman. They
refuse to recognize me as a producer. They expect you to
handle me like a silly temperamental star." Gloria Swanson
said she "would like to go on playing Sadie as long as I remain
on the screen."

JAZZ BABIES

"She was the kind of girl you'd always known, only you'd never known she was that kind of girl."*

....

In 1920, as a chubby red-haired tomboy growing up in a shabby section of Brooklyn, Clara Bow, a 15-year-old eighth-grade dropout, spent countless hours looking through movie magazines. She would daydream of slinking about in satin and ermine, sipping champagne from crystal goblets and dancing all night with worldly men who would ply her with diamonds and yard-long ropes of oversized pearls. With a psychotic one-time "working girl" mother and a perenially out-of-work father, young Clara had more reason than most girls her age to dream of leaving reality behind. But, like other girls all over the country, she had one perpetual fantasy — to live the pampered, sophisticated, pleasure-mad life that Gloria Swanson did, on-screen and off.

To girls like Clara, modern woman's rights meant that any young ingenue, if she had

long enough legs and eyelashes, could find her way to New York or Hollywood, cast away old-fashioned sexual repressions with influential men, and take a chance at being everything Gloria Swanson was. In 1920 women won the right to vote, and along with it, girls like Clara Bow could elect to wear short skirts, dance the Charleston, drink cocktails made from bootleg gin, and loosen their libidos under the moonlight while youth and good times lasted.

If you were a girl like Clara, you could even imagine getting lucky and finding your way to a millionaire's heart, or to the silver screen. After all, the movie glitterati weren't born into their titles; every movie queen alive had started out as an ordinary girl. Swanson herself, whose shoulders seemed to have been made for haute couture, who appeared to have invented Park Avenue savoir faire, had been born to the bourgeoisie. She became a star through sheer luck. In 1913, at age 14, young Gloria and her aunt visited Essanay Studios in Chicago on a day when a director just happened to need a petite dark-haired girl for a bit part—handing a bouquet to a bride. Gloria was bitten by the show-biz bug, and went on to small roles in two-reel

---

*Adela Rogers St. John, commenting on Clara Bow.

comedies. A few years later, she moved to Hollywood and became one of Mack Sennett's bathing beauties. She graduated from slapstick to a contract at Famous Players-Lasky to work with Cecil B. De Mille, who taught her all she knew about marriage among the smart set (for Swanson, that meant six husbands) and life against one opulent backdrop after another. Since De Mille used real jewels, furs, and flowers as props, Swanson was as pampered as she looked.

Girls like Clara plucked their eyebrows to Swanson-esque wisps and wore department-store copies of Gloria's beaded sheaths and plumed headdresses. Those lucky enough to have her minimalist flapper figure flaunted their flat chests. And they noticed that unlike Bara and Negri, Gloria Swanson didn't have to play — or be — a bad woman to have a terrific time, complete with multitudes of moneyed men.

With a little help from De Mille's selection of scripts, Swanson showed American women exactly what Sigmund Freud and Havelock Ellis had meant when they had warned that the repression of carnal desires lead not to virtue, but to neuroses and psychoses. By the early 1920s most of America was well-versed in some Freudian fundamentals. America now knew that even infants — not to mention post-pubescent women — had sexual responses, that any number of Freud's female patients had suffered grave physical and mental ailments as a result of denying their sexual needs, and that sexual instincts permeated every aspect of human life. Thanks to the new field of psychoanalysis, it seemed that a new kind of woman, sans corset and inevitable motherhood, had risen from the ashes of Victoriana. The new female ideal had a figure that looked boyish; no whalebone

pushed up her breasts or pinched her waist. She seemed built for driving fast cars and undulating her limbs to a jazz beat, not for making and nurturing babies.

Anyone who doubted that old-fashioned righteousness got a woman nowhere needed look no further than *The Affairs of Anatol*, released in 1921, starring Swanson as the socialite wife who didn't believe in patient devotion. Wally Reid played her husband, Park Avenue gadabout Anatol DeWitt Spencer. Though Swanson thought his behavior on the set was weird and his passes at her unwelcome, his morphine habit hadn't caught up with him yet, and he still seemed like a ripe target for the salacious new woman. And there were women galore in Anatol's life — one to match every stereotype of the day, at least on the surface.

The movie's jazz girl, Emilie Dixon (Wanda Hawley), wears fringe and feathers at the the Green Fan club, but Anatol recognizes her as his eighth-grade sweetheart, and remembers her in gingham, with an apple instead of a champagne flute at her lips. He wants to save her from the debauched life she's leading, with a rich old lecher to supply her with jewels, a plush domicile and late nights at the Green Fan. The story that she tells Anatol in flashback is a familiar one. She

---

Manhandled
Clara Bow was known as the "It" girl and the "Brooklyn Bonfire." *Manhandled* was a silent film with Gloria Swanson. This Paramount campaign book promoted *Manhandled* with Bow but due to illness, Claudette Colbert made the film renamed *Manslaughter* in 1931. An expert on the 1920s, F. Scott Fitzgerald said, "it is rather futile to analyze flappers, they are just girls...their one common trait being that they are young things with a splendid talent for living. Clara Bow is the quintessence of what the term flapper signifies: pretty, impudent, superbly assured as worldly wise, briefly clad and hardboiled as possible."

was a small-town girl looking for stardom in the big city, she'd pawned everything and acquired nothing but holes in her shoes by the time she applied for a job in the old man's office. Emilie, a perky bobbed blonde who only pretends to throw her ill-gotten jewels off the bridge when Anatol demands that she reform, turns out to have a greedy little heart underneath the gold-digging exterior. Anatol thinks he can have her love and devotion, but the old sugar daddy understands that her affection can be bought with baubles.

After a brief roll in the hay with a country girl who is more interested in picking Anatol's pocket than in falling in love, he becomes disillusioned with women who appear to be good. He pays a call on a professional vixen — Satan Synne, the Wickedest Woman in New York, played by Bebe Daniels. This vamp, however, is not what she appears to be. She may have a spider web over her dressing table, but all she really wants to drain from Anatol is $3,000, a small price to pay for reclining with a Vampire Woman. Satan Synne is a good girl in disguise, ready to sacrifice anything to pay for an operation to save the wounded soldier boy she loves.

Tired of pursuing illusions, Anatol goes home to his wife, only to find that she's been painting the town with his best friend, Max. Because Swanson as the wife has no reason to sit around waiting for an unfaithful husband

to return, she's been having as much fun at the Green Fan as Emilie has, but with a younger, handsomer escort. It takes a Hindu hypnotist to send her back to her husband.

In real life, Swanson became one of the early Hollywood stars to learn that even with morality clauses in every contract, with a minimum of discretion a star could entertain a virtually endless string of lovers. The tabloids, however, weren't so discreet, keeping Swanson's active social life in the public eye. In 1922, when her rich and balmy shoe magnate stepfather, Matthew Burns, died, rumors and the irate Burns children accused the glamour queen of having vamped the old gent into believing, in his fuzzy mental condition, that he was marrying Gloria rather than her mother, then coaxing him into leaving the bulk of his $100,000 estate to her mother. That brouhaha eventually fizzled out, but for decades fans wondered did she or didn't she have a long-term affair with Joe Kennedy — *the* Joe Kennedy, Boston banker and patriarch of the clan. The long-awaited answer in Swanson's autobiography? Yes.

As it happened, the affair was a direct result of the role she coveted most — that of Sadie Thompson, prostitute in exile on Pago Pago, from Somerset Maugham's short story "Miss Thompson," which had been Broadway's hottest hit of the 1922-1923 season as the play *Rain*, starring Jeanne Eagels.

Swanson broke her contract with Famous Players-Lasky in 1926 because she had had it with playing clotheshorses-on-a-lark. She formed her own production company, with United Artists distributing her movies. In search of a solid, earthy script, she brainstormed with director Raoul Walsh. With a blush and grin, he said, "Well, there's

Rain
Censors objected to using the word rain in a title and wouldn`t allow the razor (the suicide instrument) in the film. Joan Crawford left MGM for the first time and really didn't want to play Sadie. During the shooting, she was unhappy and stayed in her room listening to Bing Crosby records. At a welcoming dinner in Catalina a man responded to her discussion of *Rain* by announcing, "Listen fishcake, when Jeanne Eagels died, *Rain* died."

always *Rain*."

Rain was at the top of the list of the Formula, the current Motion Picture Producers and Directors Association guidelines on what not to produce. Under Will Hays's ever-vigilant eye, the association had agreed to name names of certain novels and plays that were too blatantly indecent to turn into movies. What was digestible on Broadway could be blasphemous in Hollywood, especially in the case of *Rain*, which called for Sadie to be raped by a missionary whose lust gets out of hand.

But talking it over with Walsh and her hubby number three, the Marquis Henri de la Falaise de la Coudraye, Swanson noted that the Formula made no mention of short stories, and a brilliant idea occurred to her.

She and Henri invited Hays and a few business associates to their mansion for lunch. Gloria casually took Hays aside and told him about a classic short story by a respected British author in which a clergyman loses control and commits suicide. "If I were to change him to a lay reformer, do you think it would be possible to make the story into a movie?" she asked innocently. Hays, in what she called his reedy Indiana twang, agreed.

But the shooting turned out to be so expensive that Swanson put her Malibu property on the market to try to climb out of debt. Paramount executive Bob Kane told her that she might try another option—his friend the banker, Joe Kennedy. Try him she did. In New York she lunched with a man who looked like a self-made working-class Irish millionaire to her. His Boston accent amused her when he told her he'd studied business at "Hahvahd" and then discovered that Hollywood could use his talents as financier. He was savvy about show business, and asked her how she'd ever been able to talk Hays into permitting her to do Sadie Thompson.

"I just invited him to lunch and asked him," she replied. When Kennedy laughed uproariously at the idea, she was mortified. "Latent in the joke seemed to be the implication that I'd vamped Will Hays by pressing my lips into a bee sting and batting my eyelashes," she wrote later.

That lunch led to a business partnership, and a double life for Swanson in which she was both marquess and mistress.

While Swanson and Kennedy were carrying on their secret trysts at a Beverly Hills house on ultra-swank Rodeo Drive, in another part of the neighborhood, Clara Bow was living in a simpler dwelling but showing a steady stream of men that the frisky "It" girl of the screen was but a tame version of the real Clara Bow, the sex symbol of the era.

When the matronly looking but racy-minded British novelist Elinor Glyn said that only a chosen few had "It"—she named Antonio Moreno, Rex the Wild Stallion, a doorman at the Ambassador Hotel, and Clara Bow—she meant some kind of magnetic force. "It" was more complex than sex appeal, Madame Glyn insisted. Glyn had become Hollywood's high priestess of allure by the mid-1920s. She published a story called "It" in *Cosmopolitan*, trying to clear up the confusion once and for all. "To have 'It' the fortunate possessor must have that strange magnetism which attracts both sexes.... He or

---

Sadie Thompson
Will Hays hired lip readers to tell him what was being said. Censors objected to a scene of Sadie telling the reverend (who had already been changed to a mister): "You'd yank the wings off butterflies and claim you were saving their soul, you psalm-singing son of a bitch."

Louise Brooks in a photo from the French film *Prix de Beauté*. German director Pabst discovered Louise and told her she was "a born whore." Louise was very articulate and said about herself: "I was always a kept woman...but I never had anything to show for it. I just wasn't equipped to spoil millionaires in a practical far-sighted way."

she must be entirely unself-conscious, and full of self-confidence, indifferent to the effect he or she is producing....There must be physical attraction, but beauty is unnecessary," she explained.

"It" must have been responsible for Bow's improbable rise from daydreamer to star, which began when she entered her picture in a Fame and Fortune Beauty Contest advertised in one of her favorite fan magazines in 1922, when she was 17. For most young girls who dreamed of being

Gloria Swanson, this kind of contest was nothing but wasted postage at worst, and a ticket to the down-and-out-and-disillusioned side of Hollywood at best. But for Clara, it (or was it "It"?) led to a lucky break, and a contract with B. P. Schulberg (who was known for propositioning every actress who passed his way). Lecherous studio brass or not, the new starlet was happy simply to have escaped from her tormented home in Brooklyn. Just before she had taken off for Lotus Land, she'd had to fend off her own mother, who woke her up one night with a kitchen knife at her throat, telling her, "You'd be better off dead than in show business."

Whatever Bow might have become had she stayed in Brooklyn, as a rising young star, she took the genre of modern young adventuress and gave it a mad rush of libidinous piquancy. She carried on the tradition that Swanson and Colleen Moore had started, playing tempestuous bobbed-haired ingenues who lived for pleasure and lost all reserve when a jazz band played the music born in old Storyville, but turned out to be only a little bit promiscuous.

The bad-good girl was partially a creation of the writer Samuel Hopkins Adams, who used the nom de plume Warner Fabian to write a trashy novel about the wild young generation, titled *Flaming Youth*. It told all about "the highly speeded-up life of a set craving for and feeding on excitement... representative of a society that must find some direction for its mad, goalless chase," the ads for the book proclaimed. Colleen Moore gave the creation life. Girls across the country cut their hair into straight, glossy bobs and cast away their long skirts when they saw her playing Patricia the flapper in the movie. But the celluloid vision of the mad, goalless set provided a clear outline for flapper morality; a rich jazz girl can dance and drink with the fellows all night, but when her virtue is actually threatened she has to protect herself. In Patricia's case, she saves herself from ruin at the hands of an old rake by plunging from a yacht. In short, the jazz baby could look and act like a loose woman as long as she was pure underneath and had Daddy's money on her side.

Bow's roles repeatedly instructed the flapper on how to keep herself marriageable. In *The Wild Party*, the unscholarly "It" girl played a coed who became mixed up in a scandalous party. Her reputation was ruined until the anthropology professor who had fallen in love with her cleared her name. In *Dancing Mothers*, she was less pure of heart, as a flapper named Kittens who falls for a playboy who is also turning his charms on her long-suffering mother, who in the end abandons her selfish husband and daughter. When Kittens pours down a flask of bootleg gin, her 100-watt eyes and shimmying hips give the impression that this little number is uncontrollable, but the camera never actually catches her in the act.

As a working-class flapper though, Bow seemed to find virtue a little harder to come by. In *It* she is a ribbon clerk out to hook the man who owns the department store. "I'll take the snap out of your garters!," she promises him. Of course, since Madame Glyn had written the story to illustrate what It was all about, the shopgirl with It had to get her man, even after behaving like a tart aboard his yacht. As Bubbles in *Red Hair*, which had a sequence in Technicolor so that young women could see the color to buy for their now-curly bobs, she was clearly digging for gold. As a manicurist with hot pants in *Mantrap* she marries a slow-witted oaf from the desolate Canadian woods on impulse, runs off with her husband's lawyer friend, and can't take her eyes off some new young hunk even when she makes a stab at virtue in the end.

In a homespun flannel shirt and skirt in *Mantrap*, she still managed to show the tops of her stockings. Bow's scriptwriters and directors were instructed to get her into as many situations as possible that required her to appear in bathing suits and lingerie and other stages of undress. The lingerie industry had her to thank for a boost in sales of clingy nightgowns, slips, and "scanties."

In private, rumor had it that she stripped down to even less for a game of nude touch football with the University of Southern California football team on her front lawn. Other men on her lengthy list of lovers and one-nighters included Gilbert Roland, Victor Fleming, Gary Cooper, Eddie Cantor, Bela Lugosi, and Fredric March as well as stuntmen, pilots, and men off the street. Hollywood's real trend-setting crowd, those with regular invitations to San Simeon, where William Randolph Hearst and Marion Davies reigned, considered Bow trashy. As part of that smart set, John Gilbert was nevertheless not above accepting invitations to private dalliances with her.

In her movies, Bow was always in search of true love and marriage. She was not so well-behaved in real life. When Robert Savage, a Yale football player, attempted suicide by slashing his wrists because Clara wouldn't marry him, her response was, "He's gotta be kiddin'!" Later in her life, after her one-time secretary's revelations about her sex life had **virtually ruined her popularity,** after she'd been named as a co-respondent in a divorce suit, after she had settled down to rocky matrimony, Bow, who once had seven auburn chows to match her hair, reflected on her life.

Sally, Irene and Mary
Constance Bennett, Joan Crawford, and Sally O'Neil are fun-loving flappers. Joan Crawford was friendly with Sally O'Neil but always addressed Constance Bennett as Miss Bennett. F. Scott Fitzgerald also said: "Joan Crawford is doubtless the best example of the flapper, the girl you see at smart nightclubs...dancing deliciously, with wide hurt eyes." Later, when he was trying to write for her, he said, "She has to go through a Dr. Jekyll and Mr. Hyde contortion to change the look on her face."

"The more I see of men, the more I like dogs," she said.

When an aging Louise Brooks recalled her life to Kenneth Tynan, she said something similar: "As a matter of fact, I've never been in love." But in her flapper heyday, Brooks, like Bow, gladly exchanged sexual favors with myriad men in return for a decade's worth of good times. The fact that most of the men she bumped into happened to have the power to get her into the movies and the bucks to support her was mostly coincidental, of secondary importance to her quest for fun, but it did make the raven-haired beauty from Kansas City a star.

Brooks left the prairie and became a dancer with the avant-garde Denishawn Dancers while still a teenager. She was fired for lacking commitment and got hired by Flo Ziegfeld. She frequently played hooky from Ziegfeld's shows to go out and have a good time, which annoyed her fellow chorus girls no end. She wasn't out to become an actress, but since her on-and-off affair with Paramount honcho Walter Wanger presented her with a number of opportunities to audition, she figured why not try it. After she showed her natural talent in a couple of small movie roles in 1925, Paramount and MGM both offered her contracts. Wanger advised his paramour to take the MGM contract, because if she went with his studio everyone would assume that it was due to having bedded him. Ever defiant, she took the Paramount offer.

Brooks, with her untamed exuberance and black-lacquer bob, was another natural for the quasi-wanton flapper role, which by the late 1920s seemed to be pieced together with recycled parts. In *Love 'Em and Leave 'Em* she played a shop girl who seduces her big sister Evelyn Brent's beau, fakes tears by dabbing

her cheeks with water from a goldfish bowl, and in the end, sweeps off in a Rolls Royce with the owner of the department store. However, something about Brooks—perhaps a sly vampiness in the way she batted her eyelashes and an inherent talent for behaving naughtily with absolutely no remorse—led to kinkier roles. On loan to Fox Studios, she made *A Girl in Every Port* in 1928, with Howard Hawks as writer/director, playing a gold-digging circus acrobat who comes between two sailors who think they're the ultimate womanizers until she turns the tables on them. In this movie she forsook flapper fringe for tights and sequined panties, and got to fondle Robert Armstrong's thigh while his buddy, Victor McLaglen, knelt at her feet and cleaned her shoes. After making that movie she fled to Washington with a new lover, George Marshall, a millionaire in the laundry business, having just divorced her first husband. But Hollywood caught up with her, as did a cable from Germany.

The German director G.W. Pabst wanted her, to the great consternation of all the available European actresses, to play Lulu, the remorseless coquette, the nymphomaniacal streetwalker, the temptress who overtakes her lovers like a flame leaping out of the inferno. The movie, *Pandora's Box*, gave Brooks the role for which she is best remembered. Lulu, among other travesties, marries an old man and accidentally shoots him on her wedding night, escapes to London as a fugitive with the old man's smitten son and a downtrodden former lover as companions, works the streets of the rancid East End to make ends meet, and invites handsome but penniless Jack the Ripper up to her room. When Jack, who can't help himself, thrusts a breadknife into her, death in the throes of lust is not punishment for her evil

Anna Christie
Eugene O'Neill's great American drama starring
Blanche Sweet.

deeds, as Hays might have demanded had this
been an American movie, but Lulu's ultimate
erotic experience.

In reality, after Brooks had a fling with
Gustav Diessl, the actor who played Jack the
Ripper, and then one with Pabst, played a
brothel inmate in Pabst's *Diary of a Lost Girl*
in 1930, and a beauty contest winner who is
killed by a possessive husband in the French
film *Prix de Beauté* the same year, she went

back to Hollywood and worried that she might actually become a call girl if she hung around and watched her career decline. It wasn't that she couldn't do talkies. She had a lovely voice, but everyone knew she was uncooperative. Harry Cohn tried to get her cooperation by promising her a contract with Columbia in a series of meetings in his office in which he always appeared shirtless—ready in case she decided to capitulate to his terms. Instead, she tried a few paltry roles, but left Hollywood for good in the late 1930s. A certain millionaire broadcasting executive apparently kept her on a pension for a time.

The new woman could be ambitious for far more than pleasure and eternal youth. *Time* magazine, heralding the May 1924 congress of the American Women's Association, stated that those women attending would include "15 mayors, six explorers, and 41 technical engineers. In addition, women writers, brokers, stock raisers, architects, undertakers, engravers, jewelers, doctors, farmers, editors, laywers, and clerics." It was still news when a woman succeeded in one of these male-dominated fields, but young Billie Cassin, from the poor side of Kansas City, had other ideas about how to make headlines. Everything she did was calculated to set her on the road to fame and fortune, starting with the job she took in her teens as a domestic at a ritzy girls' school. There she talked the headmistress into letting her sit in on classes. She acquired enough deportment to date

Anna Christie
Blanche Sweet stated: "The book I studied very carefully. They would use subtitles from the play, you didn't mouth very much in silent films because a mouth opening and closing is not interesting. The less you said and the more you looked. That was more important than opening and closing your mouth on lines."

some rich boys who mistook her for a
student.

From chambermaid she worked her way
through a string of menial jobs to dancer in
the "dirty" Lionel West Photoplays produced
for vending machine distribution. From
dancing nude she went on to dance in skimpy
sequined garments on the sleaze-joint circuit
in Chicago, where the job description usually
required her to mingle with customers when
she wasn't bumping and grinding on stage.
Stage-door Johnnys of a sort stood in line
after hours to mingle more closely with the
dancers. In the early 1920s, Billie had to
recover from VD and a series of botched
abortions before J.J. Shubert discovered her.
(Legend has it that she knocked a glass of
water into the theater mogul's lap at the
Oriole Terrace in Detroit and made it to
Broadway.) As a chorus girl on the Great
White Way, she wanted to be a great hoofer.
She had her dates — and there were many of
them — take her to speakeasies in Harlem,
where the Charleston was born in a show
called *Runnin' Wild*. She learned to knock her
knees with the best of them, and as a dancer
and intimate acquaintance of Harry Rapf, an
MGM exec who was paying most of her
expenses, she acquired a contract as a bit
player, even though her first screen test was a
bomb.

MGM chieftans thought the name she was
using at the time, Lucille LaSueur (LaSueur
being the name of a mysterious French
Canadian actor she'd always believed was her
real father), was too stagey, so they conducted
a Name the Starlet contest. That was how she
ended up with the name Joan Crawford, a
name she had to get used to. At first, Billie
thought it sounded squirmy, like crawdads.
But it did have a nice ingenue ring, apropos
of the youthful ambience of the era. Many

What Price Glory
In this big war movie where the men flirt, sneer, and fight
throughout the whole film, Victor McLaglen and Edmond
Lowe fight over Carmen of the Philippines. She looks like she
wishes they would make up their minds quickly. At the
premiere in New York City there was a stage prologue in
which bombs exploded, machine guns clattered, and the
scenery toppled with red flares illuminating the theatre.

years later, a plastered-looking Crawford would tell Merv Griffin and all of his viewers that she came in at the end of the silents. In fact, the silent screen was the laboratory that created her.

Since the modern age called for lean ladies, the new improved Billie Cassin obligingly acquired a gaunt look, with facial inclines that could cast their own shadows, after studio execs instructed her to go on a high-protein diet. By the late 1920s she had perfect lanky limbs, so her dancing legs, doing the Charleston in a triple mirror, became the stars of the opening sequence of *Our Dancing Daughters*. That was a hint that "Diana the Dangerous," the yacht-hopping flapper she played, was going to be another debutante in hot pursuit of pleasure. In typical pedigreed-flapper fashion, Diana turned out to be just another girl-next-door who won't be mistress to a married man no matter how much she loves him. The silver screen's nick-of-time happy ending came to the rescue once again. Lucky Diana gets handsome, rich Johnny Mack Brown at the end after his besotted, gold-digging wife slips on a stairway and tumbles drunkenly to her death.

Crawford, in real life the perfect Cinderella story of bad-girl-makes-good with the help of a few Prince Charmings, also played a less successful version of her early self from time to time. In *Sally, Irene and Mary*, she and co-stars Constance Bennett and Sally O'Neil played three Broadway chorines in search of love and stardom. Sally (Bennett), is panning for diamonds, but Crawford, as Irene, is the one who gives away her virtue too readily. The audience witnesses her folly when she appears in a lounging robe in the presence of Paul, the man she loves. A blazing fireplace says the rest. When Paul considers her unfit for holy wedlock, Irene marries someone else,

and the bride and groom are killed in a car accident. Thus she is punished for an impropriety to which only poor girls seemed vulnerable in the jazz age—at least according to the camera's eye.

In reality it was more likely that rich girls, like movie stars, had easier access to private quarters, contraceptives, and abortions than poor girls. But as Louise Brooks, the midwestern lawyer's daughter, exemplifies, if you were a young modern woman you didn't have to come from the underclass to find yourself in need of financial aid if you'd left home to seek fortune and adventure in the big city. In the real-life night-time hideaways, any number of would-be actresses and out-of-work chorus girls were able to make a buck by serving illegal liquor and intimate favors. Presumably there was always the hope of meeting some influential customer who thought you had a certain irresistible "It," but more likely, the closest you would come to stardom would be by reading fan magazine facts and fictions about Joan Crawford and her humble beginnings.

In 1929, a writer named George E. Worthington traveled undercover through the speakeasies of New York with the Committee of Fourteen, a body of prominent men and women who were taking "a modern, unemotional and scientific approach to an age-old problem," a problem their nocturnal outings found still flourished in abundance. Worthington's exposé on prostitution in the city appeared in a magazine called *The Survey*. The Committee had learned that, "the cover of secrecy necessary in dispensing synthetic gin or bootleg whiskey is cloaking still less reputable activities....Apparently illicit liquor is not enough to keep many of these enterprises going in fierce competition with each other, and still more primitive entertainment is provided on demand or almost forced on their patrons." So much for the demise of the red light district; the new speakeasies/bordellos were sprinkled all over town. Worthington described the investigators' excursion to a brownstone club in a residential section of West 71st Street. They were ushered into a room at the back of the entry hall, where there were tables with men and women drinking and a space for dancing. "The proprietor suggested that the men meet a couple of 'hostesses'. Upon their assent, he telephoned, and shortly two attractive young women arrived. Further investigation revealed that the place, innocent appearing as it seemed, instead of being a night club as they supposed, was a speakeasy house of prostitution. There were bed rooms on the upper floors and the two 'hostesses' were call-prostitutes."

The investigation turned up any number of showgirls from Broadway who were moonlighting as hostesses. "These girls get no pay during the four weeks that a production is under rehearsal, when they are required to be at the theatre practically all day. If they lack money to tide them through until it opens, night clubs offer one of the few chances for a job in the remaining house of the day....Women are also employed in the night clubs in several perfectly legitimate capacities — as singers, dancers, or members of a revue and as checkroom and cigarette girls. Sometimes these, too, are called upon to act as part-time hostesses," Worthington wrote. Moviemakers, whether investigating undercover or not, readily observed that any woman working as a showgirl or in a nightclub was of suspect reputation.

For those girls who weren't as enterprising as Billie Cassin, the future rarely held any promise but getting older and sinking lower,

like old Marthy, the lady of the waterfront in *Anna Christie*, the Eugene O'Neill play, that, as a 1923 movie starring the angelically beautiful Blanche Sweet as the whore in need of rescue, gave life to a sub-genre of bad girls for the jazz age — the Gin-Soaked Gamine Gone to Seed.

Worthington found a number of potential real-life Anna Christies who had started their careers in speakeasies. Nineteen-year-old Jean was serving a sentence in a reformatory at her own request. "You don't know how deadening it was, to drink that rotten stuff for hours and hours every night. I lost my health. I constantly had indigestion and headaches, and I didn't care what happened to me. Finally I decided that it would be better for me if I chose my own customers rather than letting the nightclub proprietor pick them out for me .... So I quit and made arrangements with a bell-boy in the hotel where the men had been taking me after the club closed, but I couldn't get my health back. I felt so rotten that the money I made didn't do me any good. I couldn't enjoy anything. I decided to give myself up to see if I would get any help by being put in an institution."

What happened to Jean is anyone's guess. She may have changed her life, or she may have ended up working in a seedier part of town. She may have found a husband she could rely on for support, or she may have become a policewoman, or a typist, or a salesclerk. (Even Louise Brooks did a stint behind the counter at Saks Fifth Avenue after the good times ended.) Olga, on the other hand, a Russian immigrant who "could sing a little and dance a little bit less," fled when the club where she worked was raided, and became a fugitive. Diane, another fugitive, had gone into the life as a teenager, when her father died suddenly and she needed a job. In

the winter of 1928 she was arrested in a raid on an apartment where she and five other girls were found staging a "circus." Diane had forfeited her bail and disappeared. As prostitutes on the lam, it would have been hard for Diane and Olga to find jobs outside the nether-strata of the demimonde.

It was at that point, after she'd fled a police raid or two and hardened her psyche to a

Lady of the Pavements
Lupe Velez plays a dancer bad-girl. She had a contract with United Artists which forbade her to indulge in strenuous diets or reducing exercises as she was curvy. The producers spent $13,500 on gowns and $4,650 on accessories. The electric bill was $7,118, about the cost of 237,266 families eating pot roast according to the film's publicity.

deeply jaded hue, that moviemakers, like the Maughams and O'Neills who came before them and inspired many of the classic Gin-Soaked Gamines of the cinema, loved to pick up on the GSG's life. Perhaps expecting as much public outrage as Camille had provoked in the previous century, the Ince Studio issued a publicity release for *Anna Christie* that hyped, above all, the movie's sophistication: "The age which has produced flappers, social and political revolutions, gland rejuvenation, radios, the jazz craze and world-wide unrest no longer can be coddled with fairy tales." In fact, *Anna Christie* was one movie that wouldn't hold up as a fairy tale, in spite of the fact that roughneck Matt — no Prince Charming himself — decides that Anna deserves redemption from her life in "one of those houses" and plans to marry her. Anna's father, Chris Christopherson, left his wife and children for "dat old devil sea." Since Matt and Chris are both about to take off for the sea at the end, a big question remains: Can Anna find happiness with a sailor, any more than her mother could?

Nevertheless, marriage is Anna's reward for wanting to be good, and for exposing society's hypocrisies by virtue of simply being a bad girl who's pure inside. Sadie Thompson is a walking exposé of the the missionary/reformer Alfred Atkinson's hypocritical lust, and at the end of the movie, she gets to sail off to Australia with Handsome O'Hara of the U.S. Marines, her new fiancé. The bad-good girl of the 1920s looked as though she wanted to do things that she didn't do; then there was the good-bad

girl who didn't want to do the things she did do, but she had to earn a living somehow. She was an old literary device dating at least as far back as Camille, and she was a natural for the jazz age. If you thought modern, what handier measure was there of the fuddy-duddy oldsters' forked-tongue approach to sexual matters than the world's oldest profession?

In William De Mille's ultramodern 1924 movie, *The Fast Set*, Zasu Pitts played a streetwalker who was invited to Adolphe Menjou's respectable home for a dinner party, as bookish Menjou's way of teaching his gadabout wife, played by Betty Compson, a lesson. She's become bored with her husband's literary crowd and has cultivated a new group of friends from the party set. When she and her friends won't speak to the hooker who comes to dinner, Menjou points out, "I never heard of an amateur billiard player refusing to play with a professional."

Over and over, the Gin-Soaked Good-Bad Girl turned out to be wearing her sexy swagger, her slinky chemises and her feather boas just to earn a living. Even Lillian Gish played a good-bad role — in *The Enemy*, in 1927, in which she was a war widow who had no other means to pay for a half-gallon of milk for her baby. She didn't want to play the role, but MGM insisted. Said Gish: "I hope this won't ruin my career."

The Good-Bad Girl frequented the waterfront and foreign war zones in Great War nostalgia pictures. She was also an essential part of any picture that dealt with the au courant "mob scene" that had grown up with side-by-side with Prohibition. In *Underworld* (1927), Evelyn Brent was a gangster's mistress who left a trail of feathers from her flashy ensembles everywhere she went and wanted nothing more than a little

---

The Enemy
In this film, Lillian Gish is forced into working briefly as a prostitute, saying, "I would do anything for a quart of milk for my baby." Here she consults with her baby's doctor. Ms. Gish disavows making this film.

UNDERWORLD

dignity. "Feathers," as she is called, is deeply wounded when she tries to make the intellectual mobster named Rolls Royce think she's reading a book, and he turns it right side up for her.

When Hollywood recalled men who had shown their courage on distant battlefields, the scenario often had room for a woman who could display her heroism by making her own brand of sacrifice. In *The Woman Disputed* (1928), Norma Talmadge is Mary Ann, the heroic hooker. Her own battle begins with a love triangle. She must choose between Lieutenant Nika Turgenov of the Russian army and his friend Lieutenant Paul Hartman of the Austrian army. When she picks Paul, Nika becomes her private enemy. After a complicated maze of war subterfuges and machinations, Mary, now an ambulance driver, is among a group of four prisoners taken by a Russian unit commanded by none other than Nika, now a captain. When Captain Turgenov sentences her companions to immediate execution, Mary makes a Faustian deal with her jilted suitor: her body in exchange for the lives of the three prisoners. When Paul returns from battle and hears of what she has done, he threatens to break off their engagement. Not until

10,000 men kneel at her feet and beg her forgiveness for what war made her do does Paul realize the pettiness of his jealousy and the nobility of her act.

Betty Compson, as a lady of the waterfront in *The Docks of New York*, finds a low-born seaman of low moral character and redeems him with her pure heart. Bill the burly stoker (George Bancroft), ashore on an eight-hour leave and ripe for adventure, rescues her from trying to drown herself and marries her in a fake ceremony. While The Girl (as Compson's character is known) is sleeping contentedly, believing that at last a man has made her "decent," he sneaks out. In a scene that was cut from many prints of the movie, he leaves some money on her bedside table, re-counts the money, reconsiders, and leaves her a little more before he walks out on her. And yet she continues to trust him. When he learns that she's in trouble, first for shooting Bill's commander when he tries to rape her, then for the theft of the clothes that Bill stole for her after he pulled her from the harbor, Bill gets painful pangs of conscience which grow stronger as the movie wears on. By the end, he accepts his year-long sentence for

---

ABOVE, LEFT: *Underworld*
This tale about a Chicago gunman and his moll, Feathers McCoy, began the gangster film genre. Feathers were a visual clue to the audience that the woman was bad. "You have to be bad to be good. No younger sister or daughter of mine would ever get into films if I had any influence," Ms. Brent commented.

OPPOSITE: *Lady of the Night*
Norma Shearer leads a double life. Norma Shearer said, "My first feeling was one of joy at the opportunity of playing both of the feminine leads — the most overwhelming feeling was what I would do with both parts so diametrically opposed." Shearer smoked Melachrino cigarettes and if you bought 12 boxes you would get a free ticket to the movie. It was Joan Crawford's first part as she doubled for her.

theft, and promises to be a good husband when he gets out.

Because she was always a humanitarian, the Gin-Soaked Gamine was more widely known—is still widely know—by her more popular and all-embracing title, the Prostitute with a Heart of Gold. Samuel Goldwyn is reputed to have perused a first-draft script and shouted "Get me a P with an H of G!" more than once. Hollywood didn't invent the P with an H of G, but without her, the celluloid bad girl might have become an endangered species.

What made her so essential? Frederick James Smith analyzed that question in *Photoplay* in the 1920s. For one thing, he said, women sympathized with her and could identify with her, as they never had with the vamp.   That was important to the box office because audiences were by then as much as 75% female. "Woman," wrote non-feminist Smith, "through moral restrictions dating back through the ages, has had to seek vicarious experience. In other words, woman has had to gain adventure second hand.... It is human — and distinctly feminine, as well — to substitute one's self for a heroine of a printed or an enacted romance. Students of femininity declare that all women, sometime in their life, want to play at being bad; to be the center of an adventure without danger to themselves. Thus, the feminine portion of an

West of Zanzibar
Mary Nolan, "the hard luck girl," had been the toast of Ziegfeld Follies, hence the name Bubbles. It took a move to Germany to be discovered by Hollywood. Her private life was devastating she was a battered wife and once sued an MGM executive for assault. In this film, she plays a drug addict hooked on opium and booze, but in real life she was on morphine.

audience admires feminine sex appeal on the screen when it isn't too blatant. That is, sex appeal that is only fooling. To be successful, film sex appeal in an actress must not offend women."

And even more important, Will Hays, like the reverend-turned-lay-reformer who couldn't resist Sadie Thompson, had a special affection for the P with an H of G. Smith saw an unwritten moral code between the lines of the Formula, and concluded that a movie couldn't depict a woman who was promiscuous and enjoyed it. "Yet the screen frequently shows a young woman being forced into immorality, either through physical force or to get money for a sick relative. Yet the films cannot show immorality as a moral weakness or a psychological case," he said. As long as she was in it for economic need, not for a good time, she could be as active as a scriptwriter's imagination allowed.

That is why rich girls simply didn't. Unless, of course, one was talking about the real life of one who had earned a small fortune playing the role of bad-good girl time and again. After the stock market crashed, the nation's economy fizzled out, and a series of nervous breakdowns precluded any further acting assignments for Clara Bow, Daisy DeVoe did talk about the real life of Bow, her former employer. Daisy talked in court, after Bow had noticed her money supply disappearing and sued her former secretary for embezzling some $30,000 from her bank accounts. Daisy had been keeping a log of the men who entered Clara's boudoir. Daisy went to prison for a year, but the consummate jazz baby, like the jazz age itself, lost her effervescence almost overnight.

The flapper had a short lifespan, it turned out. The country was unsympathetic to Bow's brand of sexual enlightenment; she'd

The Woman Disputed
Norma Talmadge said, "The public is more tolerant as there is greater interest today in the hard realities of life. The only thing that interested me is the story behind a gal, her background, her reason to be whatever she is so long as she is interesting." In the movie, the leading man offers her money and she refuses. As a prank, Norma Talmadge told the director to shoot the scene with no film and this time she accepted the money. Everyone on the set cracked up.

overdone a good thing. Besides, by the time Daisy told all, a more somber decade had arrived, and people who were struggling to ward off the Depression were aghast at the way the consummate jazz baby had simply lost track of $30,000. Bow suffered a series of little nervous breakdowns and ate bonbons. Though she married cowboy actor Rex Bell, repaired to his Nevada ranch, had two sons, and even had some of the cows dyed auburn during one of her short frolicsome spells, she would never again be either trim or carefree.

Swanson found new husbands and new business ventures, including a line of clothes and a natural cosmetic label. But it was Crawford who stayed in Hollywood, whose career as an actress—as opposed to a type— flourished. She played good women and bad women and bad-good women and good-bad women and P's with H's of G, and she even played the role of loving adoptive parent in real life. How did a one-time bad girl who turned out not to have a heart of gold at all make it? In 1931 she starred in a movie that had many parallels to her life story, *Possessed*. When Clark Gable escorts her, a small-town proletarian who has just fled a job in a cardboard box factory to take on New York, to dine atop the city, she matter-of-factly orders meat and potatoes, without even looking at the menu. "I know what I want," she says. No vamping, no Charleston rhythms, no bee-stung lips. No "It." Now a bad girl had to be brazen and practical, with a knack for acquiring cold, hard cash—quite a challenge considering that she had to have a tender heart as well. The flapper was dead, and Joan Crawford was riding the tide.

GOLDEN GODDESSES AND GOLD DIGGERS

Gone are my blues and gone are my tears
I've got good news to shout in your ears
The silver dollar has returned to the fold,
With silver you can turn your dreams to gold.

We're in the money,
We're in the money;
We've got a lot of what it takes to get along!
We're in the money,
The skies are sunny;
Old man depression, you are through,

you done us wrong!

We never see a headline
'bout a breadline today,
And when we see the landlord, we look
that guy right in the eye.

We're in the money,
Come on, my honey,
Let's spend it, lend it, send it
rolling along! 'long!*

. . . .

Mae West, who had been paying her own way since she left home to join a road company at the age of 13, learned about life on the bottom at Welfare Island Prison. She served eight days there in 1927 on a charge of

lewdness, after cops raided the billowy auteur's Broadway shocker, *Sex*, in which she played an employee of a Montreal whorehouse. Some years later, she told a *New York Sun* reporter about the prisoners she met in the waiting room when she arrived. One said she was 45, but looked 65. One was a scarred, stick of a woman who had stolen a pair of shoes and one was a consumptive derelict. About the time she had finished sizing up her companions, a man wearing a driver's cap came into the room. His job was to take inmates from the waiting room to their "guest quarters." "He was young and plenty good looking," she noted. For her, jail

---

Common Law
In this 1933 movie, a woman with a past becomes an artist's model, then threatens to leave her sugar daddy. He sneers and asks, "How can you support yourself? You'll have to come back to me."

---

wasn't quite as bad as she had expected it to be.

The next time she went to court, when New York's finest raided her production of *Pleasure Man* ("a sickening excess of filth," according to the *New York Sun*), the actors who had been cast as transvestites demonstrated the acrobatics that, on stage and in costume, exposed their true gender. The prosecuting D.A. turned apoplectic, but Mae and her sidekicks stayed out of jail. She penned a new vehicle for herself about a jezebel of the "Gay 90s," whose ill-gotten jewels are legend on the Bowery. Mae was touring in *Diamond Lil* when the stock market dropped through the ground, but she wasn't worried about her own fortunes. While even maids and shoeshine boys had bought stock in the bull market, "what money I had was in show business and my diamonds," she recalled in her memoirs. "I didn't invest in anything I couldn't sit and watch."

While breadlines formed around the country, Paramount Pictures invited the now-notorious Mae to come play a supporting role for a cushy $5,000 a week. That was 1932. Mae was in the middle of another play, *The Constant Sinner*, about a hooker mixed up with underworld kingpins and the seamy side of Harlem's speakeasies. B.P. Schulberg, soon to be ousted as head honcho at Paramount, had not personally witnessed her novel talents, but her old pal George Raft was scheduled to play a reforming gangster in a new production, and he had said, "Get Mae West." Raft knew that the two of them were naturals for this picture. After all, Mae couldn't have produced *The Constant Sinner* without George's aid — as collector for one of her behind-the-scenes underworld backers.

Mae went out to Hollywood and sat around collecting her salary while waiting for the script to be finished. When she finally saw the script, she nearly stormed off the lot and back to New York. She had paid her dues performing as directed in vaudeville, only to find out that nobody knew better than she how to utilize her busty blondeness and nasal honky-tonk songmanship. This script proved once again that only Mae West could write Mae West-ian lines. The writers had given her a bland part that any contract starlet could have played. Mae told the producer, William LeBaron, that she'd pay back all of her salary if he would set her free from Paramount. But LeBaron came up with a better offer; he told Mae that she could rewrite the part to her own specifications.

And so, Mae West's first line on the silver screen was her own concoction, now firmly etched in film lore. Her grand entrance into the cinema came as the majestically gaudy ex-mistress of ex-gangster Raft, the one who paused at the coat-check counter of Raft's speakeasy just long enough to flash her material assets. The setup was the coat-check girl's astonished, "Goodness, what beautiful diamonds!" The comeback was, of course, "Goodness had nothing to do with it, dearie."

She stole the show from Raft and the official leading lady, Constance Cummings, who played the impoverished debutante for whom Raft was willing to give up his lucrative position in the mob. It was a script for the hard times: Cummings's foreclosed old family mansion has become Raft's speakeasy because the old order is changing and aristocratic money losing its hold on the shrinking economy. And Mae West, who was shrewd enough to negotiate an extra $100,000 for her literary contributions to the script, had arrived to demonstrate one sure way to survive the Depression in diamond-studded comfort.

Skyscraper Souls
The advertisement read: "Heaven and Hell, all within the grinning steel skeleton of the world's tallest building."

Gold digging was an old sport, but it had a golden age on the Hollywood screen from 1930 until 1934, when killjoy referee Hays cracked down on the sneakier maneuvers of the game. Mae West may have been the most luminous reason behind both the golden age and the crackdown, but other enhancing factors included Garbo's wistful wantonness, Dietrich's self-mocking songbirds, Harlow's brassy luster, and the tangy wisecracks of Busby Berkeley's gang of chorus girls. Besides, the box office returns indicated that

America's workforce, 25 percent unemployed and 75 percent worried about unemployment in l932, would happily pay a little cash for a pretty fantasy.

For most of the audience, a movie in which sexy women use their wiles to get rich—not just get by, but climb into the social circles that could still afford to drink bootleg champagne every night—was pure fantasy. It was also the golden era for the age-old fantasy of any man past his prime: scrape together enough cash and buy Ginger Rogers, clad in a gold-coin bikini. As a showgirl in *Gold Diggers of 1933*, she could pan for buying power with a few historical precedents on her side. One-time showgirls Evelyn Nesbit, Betty Compton, and Hollywood's own

Marion Davies had done very well when armed with the financial assets of Stanford White, New York City Mayor Jimmie Walker, and William Randolph Hearst, respectively.

Any number of movies showed that gold digging could produce happy, wealthy endings for a girl with spunk, talent, and some clingy satin underthings. Ina Claire and Joan Blondell managed to evade marriage and sail off on their merry way to Europe in search of foreign currency in *The Greeks Had a Word for Them*. In a later age of moviemaking they would have been forced to repent and settle down, but in 1932 United Artists felt obliged to make only two concessions to morality. In the stage version a third gold-digging partner had also been

aboard the ship, but in the movie she married a rich man instead. The play's title, *The Greeks Had a Word for It*, also underwent a discreet alteration, because Elinor Glyn had taught Hays a new dirty two-letter word.

The young women in the audience were more likely to find out-of-work husbands if they found any mates at all. Unemployed bachelors had a tendency to panic over the thought of supporting a family and vanish from the potential homefront, drifting around the country in search of either work, a call to revolution, or both. The professional doors that had opened to women during the feminist wave of the 1920s shut again because a woman who held a job that a male breadwinner could fill was considered a "menace to society." That left "women's

jobs," if you could get them, as one option, and finding a prosperous husband as the other. The pool of American men with annual earnings of $1 million or more shrunk, according to government figures, from 513 in 1929 to 150 in 1930, down to 75 in 1931. It would follow that a good gold digger had to be pretty quick-witted to beat out the competition. West, as Tira the lion-tamer in the movie, *I'm No Angel*, played a recording of something called "Nobody Loves Me Like That Dallas Man" for the foil from Dallas, hiding her stash of records for "That Chicago Man," "That New York Man," et cetera. Trixie Lorraine (Aline MacMahon) in *Gold Diggers of 1933* knew how to get right to the point. "You know, I think we should take a stroll on Fifth Avenue and look at the shops.

Three Blind Mice
Three sisters inherit money and decide to go to the big city to get rich husbands. One acts like a rich woman and the other two pose as her secretary and maid. "Mingle with plumbers and you'll marry one, mingle with millionaires and you'll marry one." Loretta Young had a "swear box" on all her sets and everyone who swore was fined. A male actor kidded with her, asking, "How much for fuck?" "Nothing, that's free," she replied.

You'd be surprised at how reasonable things are these days," she says to Nathaniel Peabody of the Boston Peabodys (Guy Kibbee).

The lines were memorable, and best of all, they were spoken, or sung when the hidden meaning was too spicy for ordinary speech. The Hays Office was watching the talkies closely, but had not yet pounced upon the tone of Mae's voice, or the innuendo behind Garbo's sighs, or the Berkeley gang's lavish sex set to music. The audience knew to listen for the throwaway lines, understanding the nuance when a gossipy Rogers prattled: "She makes $45 a week and sends $100 of it home to her mother." Still, a film goddess had to have serious magnetism to show, in undertones and meaningful gazes, what Hays wouldn't allow her to actually say or do. The reigning goddesses themselves became symbols of sex on the screen, so that even when Garbo played a queen (*Queen Christina*, 1933), or a prima ballerina who "vants to be let alone" (*Grand Hotel*, 1932), the audience knew more about her character's life behind closed doors than the scriptwriter did.

With the talkies came advances in the incandescent lighting used during filming, and that allowed another innovation in goddess fashion: for the first time, a sex queen's tousled tresses could be as fair as moonlight itself. In the 1920s, fair-haired stars like Mary Pickford had received the halo treatment with backlighting. As a student at the Max Reinhardt theatrical school in Berlin, Marlene Dietrich had been told to forget

Hold Your Man
Jean Harlow as a tramp. At a prison wedding she wears denim designed by Adrian. She sings for the first time in a film. Even though she had a perfect figure, MGM demanded she wear a girdle because the satin gowns wrinkled if she didn't.

about a screen career because her blonde hair photographed dead and her blue eyes looked like Little Orphan Annie's on-screen. Blonde hair was considered "unfortunate" in the early twentieth century, when the ideal young damsel had light brown locks, but now the movies themselves brought on a whole new fashion. World War I zeppelins and clingy black negligee aside, Jean Harlow's platinum hair was the real star of *Hell's Angels*. The studio hairdresser had created it with a formula of 20-volume peroxide combined with a few drops of ammonia. Women saw her in the movie and rushed to beauty parlors demanding the same tortuous treatment. As a public service, *Photoplay* ran an article entitled "Don't go platinum yet. . . read before you dye!," explaining the whole excruciating process that Harlow, whose roots were light brown, underwent in the name of stardom. In those days a hairdresser had to strip the hair's natural color, then add a blue rinse that would stretch out even a natural wave. The job would take an entire day, and touch-ups would be required once a week—at a cost of $50 per salon visit. Eventually even Harlow had to start wearing white wigs for the camera, because her own hair was starting to turn to straw.

Was it worth the torture? In the previous decade, Anita Loos had thought so, noting during a cross-country train trip that all the men in her party had their eyes on an air-headed young blonde, although she was really no more comely than the brown-haired Loos. The book she started writing during the train ride, *Gentlemen Prefer Blondes*, gave birth to Lorelei Lee, Hollywood's prototype blonde hussy who tuned out on school midway through second-grade grammar but knows more than a mineralogist does about how to track down diamonds. Dumb-blondeness, however, turned out to be a luxury available only in affluent times; the gold-digging blonde of the depression era had to have her wits about her. Rich men seemed to respond generously to the snappy lines and quick comebacks that talkies made possible. Except for Garbo, who could gaze at life wistfully, aloof on her pedestal above the hoi polloi, a goddess-on-the-make had to be resilient and laugh at life. Like primitive man long before her, she understood that chasing her prey and his wallet was just as exhilarating as bagging him.

No one seemed to enjoy the hunt more than Mae West. Let Barbara Stanwyck finagle her way to a bank vice-president's suite (*Baby Face*, 1933); for West there would be no mundane typing jobs, no matter where they might lead. In *She Done Him Wrong*, she reincarnated Diamond Lil of the stage play by the same name, changing the title to pacify Mr. Hays, who knew of her Broadway reputation. Paramount itself was down at the heels at the time, about to sell out to MGM, but Lil, revamped as "Lady Lou, one of the finest women who ever walked the streets," saved the studio with a $2 million domestic gross. Park Avenue ladies apparently admired Lou, who could remember when the wolf pup of want and hunger came into her home and had kittens enough to stage "Lady Lou" parties, at which wide-brimmed "Gay 90s" hats were de rigeur.

Meanwhile, Mae was able to save Cary Grant for herself for two movies. When she was still minus a leading man for *She Done Him Wrong*, she spotted the best looking thing in Hollywood on the studio lot, and said, "If he can talk, I'll take him."

"Why don't you come up sometime, see me?. . . Come up, I'll tell your fortune," Lady Lou says to Grant in the movie.

Baby Face
Barbara Stanwyck said "I was forced to make *Baby Face* for glamour and I hated it." This film made Hays angry and caused Darryl Zanuck to resign as assistant to Jack Warner. Barbara Stanwyck is sold by her father, instead she runs away and vamps her way up the corporate ladder going through twelve men in the process. She commented on her

characterization: "The baby-faced vamp is coming back now, along with other prewar fashions....I don't think she ever disappeared, but she was in the background during the era of streamlined feminine figures, without hips....She won't be an exact duplicate of her sister of the 1890s and 1900s but she'll still have the same bag of tricks, the same babyish stare and cute kittenish ways, the same line of prattle, the same ingratiating helplessness that the Dresden Dolls had."

Lou also saves Sally, a young "fallen" girl, from suicide and tells her, "When women go wrong, men go right after them!" From there, however, the hand of Hays appears. Lou is unaware that her fancy man (Noah Beery, Sr.) is operating his Bowery salooon as a cover for his white slave trade and counterfeiting racket. When Beery says he'll find a job for Sally, it takes Lou some time to catch on, but when she does, she exclaims, aghast, "You mean you turned her into a...a classy burglar?"

According to the Mae West code, gold could be found in a solid hunk of muscles as readily as in a man's bank vault. Lady Lou dumps rich man Beery for poor man Grant, an undercover police officer posing as a Salvation Army missionary, and lets him replace her mammoth diamonds with a tiny stone for her left hand. However, in the scripts that followed, she wasn't above social climbing, and finding some scrumptious beefcake at the top rung. In *I'm No Angel*, Cary Grant becomes a blueblood lawyer...and when Tira has worked her way up from a dingy carnival tent to a penthouse, she apppreciates what money can get her. There are the diamonds, then there's the black maid (Hattie McDaniel) who's better than a sister to her, to whom she can say, hand posed smugly on sequined hip, "Beulah, peel me a grape!"

Garbo, on the other hand, never got to enjoy material indulgence. Titled men smothered her with jewels and fine carriages in *Camille* (a late gold-digger movie, made in 1936), but when the Baron de Varville gave her 40,000 francs, he felt it gave him license to slap her around, but her melancholy sighs said that all she really cared about was being near Armand, who earned a modest 7,000 francs a year. As Camille, as Anna Christie in

her first talkie (1930), and as the illegitimate child who is practically born "bad" in *Susan Lenox, Her Fall and Rise*, she was clearly in the business only for the money, and her beauty had only made her man's victim.

Yet, there was a time when the Great Garbo was a mere mortal who didn't have a chance in Hollywood, at least in the shortsighted eyes of Louis B. Mayer. Greta Lovisa Gustafson, daughter of a Swedish laborer, lathered men's faces in a barber shop, was an errand girl, salesclerk, and hat model before she went to drama school in Stockholm. She was stocky and athletic-looking in her first movie, the 1922 slapstick comedy *Peter the Tramp*, in which she cavorted around on the beach with two other Swedish girls, looking not at all aloof or melancholy. But a prominent director named Mauritz Stiller saw something there and made her his protégée. When Mayer offered Stiller a contract in America, he talked the mogul into a deal—he would come only if Greta came with him. "Tell her that in America men don't like fat women," retorted Mayer.

She slimmed down and seduced John Gilbert for real when they made *Flesh and the Devil* together in 1927. In the movie, a pastor tells Gilbert, "My boy, when the devil cannot reach us through the spirit, he creates a woman beautiful enough to reach us through the flesh." And Garbo appeared as a new kind of vamp—cool and golden-haired, with a 1920s' style cupid's bow mouth, and a gaze

Anna Christie
The ad for the American version blared "Garbo Speaks." Nowadays it would read "Garbo lays." Greta felt the role was "degrading to Swedes," but she did like the German version, pictured here, made three weeks later. Her make-up and acting are much more realistic in this foreign adaptation.

that was unfathomable and yearning, borne of passions that seemed to come from her own infinite, cosmic torment rather than from carnal desires. Makeup artists saw that this face was already perfectly etched, and painted her with subtlety. American women, accustomed to the war paint that Clara Bow and the vamps had used, saw for the first time that makeup could look respectable. The cosmetic industry estimated that for every one lipstick sold in 1921, 1,500 were sold in 1931. Meanwhile, the man who had brought her to Hollywood never really lit a spark there, and died brokenhearted, still in love with Greta, while she was busy making *Wild Orchids* in 1928.

Did she love Stiller? Her melancholy air came before his death. And since she was shy around people who asked nosy questions, and stayed away from the Hollywood social scene, the mystery of Garbo became her allure. Her fans felt that she was tempting them, then running away, just as she had perhaps done with Stiller. She and Gilbert produced sizzling voltage together on screen, but when they actually did run off to Mexico to elope, Garbo changed her mind halfway through the trip. She ran off the train and hid in the ladies room of the station until the train back to Los Angeles arrived. After that, they turned their heads the other way when they passed each other on the MGM lot. Later the gossip columnists were abuzz over a story that Garbo and Rouben Mamoulian had run off to get married, and were spotted checking into a hotel as Mary Jones and Robert Bonji, but wherever she might have gone with whom, Garbo returned alone. Rumors linking her with Noël Coward also failed to produce a Mr. Greta Garbo. In *Flesh and the Devil* a man could keep her—though not bind her soul—with diamonds, but in her later movies,

no man could really have her. She loved Clark Gable with masochistic devotion in *Susan Lenox*, her eyes met Robert Taylor's and the air around them seemed to pulsate in *Camille*, but Garbo's leading men always seemed like mere targets for a passion that always

boomeranged back to her own enigmatic soul. When she played a bad girl—in *Inspiration* that meant an artist's model who beds down with every bohemian on the Left Bank—there was always a man whose love for her made

TOP: Garbo in *Red Dust*
This studio pressbook from MGM touts Garbo as the star, but Thalberg decided Harlow was perfect and cancelled Garbo. John Gilbert was to be the leading man, but he was changed for Clark Gable.

OPPOSITE: Harlow in *Red Dust*
The advertisement said: "A devastating love drove them into each other's arms." Jean Harlow was 21 and her husband had just committed suicide so the script was toned down. Clark Gable called her "baby." She cried publicly at the preview of the film and later asked her agent, "What kind of whore part do I play next?"

him cruel with passion, insane with jealousy. She might sacrifice her own happiness for him, yet still, her pain seemed to come from some otherworldly depths.

But Garbo did communicate with her friends about earthly concerns. When she was cast as Anna Christie, she was concerned that her first speaking role would typecast her. "Here I learn English and now I have to practice a Swedish dialect," she complained to Marie Dressler.

Jean Harlow was one all-American girl who did marry a millionaire's son. The bride was only 16, and Chuck McGrew, a dashing 22, gave her a quarter of a million for a wedding present. But when Harlean Carpenter McGrew, who had had a pony and a country hideaway as a child, came to her senses and realized that the marriage had been an infantile infatuation, she gladly gave up the idle life to play insolvent young nymphets out to make a killing in the man market. In *Hell's Angels* she came between two brothers who caught her smooching in a cafe with yet a third man. In *Red-Headed Woman*, with her hair tinted scarlet, she worked her way up the social ladder. First she set her sights on a young small-town pillar of the community, letting him see the picture of himself in a locket on her lace garter. Then there was a rich New Yorker who sighs, "You're so beautiful. What's the use?," and

Mogambo
A remake of *Red Dust*, the new title means passion in Swahili, the dialect of the region where the film was shot. Frank Sinatra, who was married to Ava Gardner, wanted to be on location and director John Ford ordered him to cook them all a spaghetti dinner. At first Ava had trouble with Ford, as he was so gruff, until he told her, "You're damn good, just take it." The locals complained about Ava's nude bathing scene. When she heard about it, she ran all over the set nude.

finally, she drives off through the streets of Paris with a decrepit millionaire and a virile young chauffeur. In *Dinner at Eight* she has married Wallace Beery for obvious reasons that glitter all over her neck and arms, even while she's reclining between her satin sheets, but Beery never lets her forget that he found her in the Hottentot Club in Passaic, clearly the wrong side of the tracks. Yet even a gold digger could have an H of G; as Beery's wisecracking wife, who has to pay her maid in diamond bracelets to keep her from talking about the handsome doctor's housecalls, she won't let her husband cheat shipping magnate Lionel Barrymore and send him to the poorhouse. In *Red Dust* she's a real P with an H of G and something more—pizzazz. While good woman Mary Astor simpers her way to Clark Gable's private quarters on the rubber plantation, Harlow, who understands him, makes him laugh, and waits patiently for him to see past her gaudy gowns and tarty guffaws.

In the movie, Gable comes around. Since she was nursing his bullet would—courtesy of Astor, who turned out to be not such a noble lady after all—they even got to tumble in bed a little. When she wasn't making pictures, however, Harlow was trying to live down the reputation that fame and fortune and strong peroxide had brought her. Her dear grandfather had warned her about displaying

herself in skimpy satin years before, after he'd gone to the picture show in Kansas City one hot summer night, and with a gasp of horror, recognized the slender blonde in the black teddy as his beloved granddaughter. He rushed home and placed a long distance call to Beverly Hills.

"You've disgraced your family, you've disgraced our name. You've dragged us all in the dirt," he thundered. Jean, then known as Harlean Carpenter, told Hal Roach she was quitting the next day. This bit player was no great loss to Roach at the time, but Harlean got so tired of hanging around the house with Chuck, she eventually made a pact with grandpa—he would accept her playing a sex bomb, but she'd have to do without an allowance from him—and went back to the studios. The night after *Hell's Angels* was released, everyone was talking about the new "hot number."

"Change one letter in her last name and you've got the right moniker for her," Adela Rogers St. John heard someone say at Howard Hughes's post-premiere gala. Jean's mother and stepfather chaperoned her everywhere she went, and yet everyone seemed to have ideas about her. The only man who understood her as a person was MGM producer Paul Bern, an older man, dignified and cerebral, frequent father-confessor to troubled young starlets. She married him for his mind, but he turned out to have other ideas. Only several years later did the world learn, in discreetly written newspaper and fan rag accounts, that Bern had not been a "real" husband, a secret that was revealed in the autopsy following his suicide. Translation: he was impotent, and married her because he thought a sex goddess could cure his problem. When, on their wedding night, he found out she couldn't, he

---

Morocco
Marlene Dietrich accepts money for her apples. Von Sternberg, the director and discoverer of Marlene, was supposedly in love with her. In the movie her wealthy patron Adolphe Menjou is even made up to look like Von Sternberg. This was Marlene's first film made in America. She wasn't allowed to see the script, but every day Von Sternberg told her the story. The studio demanded that she lose 30 pounds, and pluck her eyebrows and then painted imitation ones on. They sprinkled her hair with gold powder. Tallulah Bankhead commented, "I'll put gold powder in my pubic hair."

beat her black-and-blue, and kicked her in the pelvis. After that, she suffered from chronic kidney damage and a goddess identity crisis. There was a man who met her cruising a bar in disguise, and told her, "You look enough like Jean Harlow to be her double." She was on an emotional recovery cycle, and happily engaged to William Powell when she died of a kidney infection that was worsened when her Christian Scientist mother hid her away and tried to cure her with prayer instead of medicine. Not all marriages to well-established older men had happy endings.

When Marlene Dietrich, playing a mysterious woman singing in a desert dive in *Morocco*, forsook the rich debonair Adolphe Menjou to follow Gary Cooper, a dashing but poor Legionnaire, across the sands of the Sahara, she proved that foreign goddesses had changed since the previous decade. Not only were they fair and Nordic instead of swarthy, but now they were also just as apt to become a man's slave as they were to be the dominatrix. Her sexual mystique, in fact, knew no bounds. In the same picture, Dietrich's Hollywood debut, she appears singing in white tie and tails, takes a flower from a woman and kisses her on the lips. To tone down the scene she throws the flower to Gary Cooper, but the seed of doubt is planted. As a matter of fact, among the many men Dietrich was rumored to have cavorted with—Maurice Chevalier, Ernest Hemingway, and, of course, her alleged Svengali Josef Von Sternberg, not to mention her Austrian husband—there was also talk linking her with a switch-hitting "Sewing Circle" that included Claudette Colbert, Lili Damita, and the lesbian writer and socialite Mercedes d'Acosta. Mercedes was, if nothing else, a close friend who encouraged Marlene to wear drag attire off-screen. She did until

women all over America noticed and started appearing in slacks, then she switched back to skirts and ruffles.

Dietrich, too, came to America under the protective wing of her European director. Von Sternberg had made her an international star in *The Blue Angel*, the story of a mild-mannered schoolteacher's obsession with the bombshell Lola Lola, a cabaret singer of sorts. Her stage career begins in an establishment in which the manager tells the girls, "You must drink. I'm not paying you for your art." The movie made Dietrich's throaty voice and vixen half-smile an institution. After that, every time she sang her throaty, suggestive cabaret songs, showed her garter belt, or fleeced a man of his money and self-respect, she seemed to be aping herself as Lola Lola. Once in Hollywood, Von Sternberg made her debauched, irresistible, and usually in need of funds, in *Morocco*, *Dishonored*, *Shanghai Express*, and *Blonde Venus* during the gold-digger era. Marlene grew accustomed to Von Sternberg's ribald touches to her mock-serious seduction techniques—but once, when she decided to see how effective Marlene Dietrich playing a fallen woman really was, she was disappointed. One day in 1932, while strolling through the Soho district of London with her friend Hans Kohn, she sauntered over to the streetwalkers' beat and began parading, with a veil over her famous face. Not one man approached her. After half an hour, she crossed the street, and told Kohn, "I'm a complete flop as a prostitute!"

THE PROFESSION THAT DARED NOT SPEAK ITS NAME

Illicit sex.
   a) Illicit sex is contrary to divine law and in a number of cases contrary to human law.
   b) Because of the natural and spontaneous reaction of normal human beings to sexual stimuli, the portrayal of definite manifestations of sex is harmful to individual morality, subversive to the interests of society and a peril to the human race.
   c) Illicit sex must not be presented as attractive.
   d) It must not be presented in such a way as to arouse passion or morbid curiosity.
   e) In general, it must not be explicit or detailed in method or manner.
   f) It must not appear to be right or permissable—must not be justified or condoned.
   g) It must not be used for comedy or farce.

Prostitution.
The Code Administration eliminates portrayal of, or reference to, prostitution wherever it has not essential relation to the plot, wherever it is presented as glamorous or enviable and wherever there is no ample compensating moral value.

The Code demands "that in the end the audience feels that evil is wrong and good is right." To satisfy this requirement of the Code, stories must contain at least sufficient good to compensate for any evil they relate. The compensating moral values are: good characters, the voice of morality, a lesson, regeneration of the transgressor, suffering, and punishment.*

---

*Excerpts from Joseph Breen's annual report to Will Hays on the activities of the Production Code Administration, March 1, 1936.

OPPOSITE: Mae West in a police station in 1926. She co-wrote a play that was intitially called *Following the Fleet* and instructed her collaborator to write a play like *Sadie Thompson* about a loose woman living off sailors, as the original used soldiers. The play about a prostitute in a brothel would have lasted well over its 375 performances, but a vice commission busted Mae and her production. When she was pinched she almost trampled a cop who asked, "What's your rush?" She replied, "Last time I had to stand" in the paddy wagon. She was fined $500 and sentenced to ten days, which was reduced to eight for good behavior. She said, "I didn't have to go to jail, but I knew they'd treat me like a society prisoner...the Warden was very nice...he used to take me out every night....He had a nice mother too...a very good cook." Mae West said thousands and thousands of young girls all over the world are prostitutes: "Most of them were innocent. In this play I presented the picture of a young girl whose great beauty and economic poverty forced her into bad ways. *Sex* has educational value because it shows the life and psychology of a prostitute."

When two Catholic priests came to call on Mae West shortly after *I'm No Angel* was released, she couldn't help but notice that one of them was quite handsome. If she imagined him without his clerical robes, though, he had other ideas. The handsome one got right to the point: the Church was worried about Mae West's influence on its flock. "A woman told me in the confessional," he reported, " 'Father, I have sinned. I've committed adultery. It was that Mae West movie that drove me to it.'"

Mae West was not singlehandedly responsible for the Legion of Decency and the Production Code, but her lion-whip certainly spurred the nation's zealots to action. What they seemed to fear most was her bottom line at the box office. As one reformist writer railed:

"Tho they are sweating over the scrubbrush now, the movie-makers can scarcely avoid wondering whether the larger part of their public really relishes what the church folk call wholesome themes half so much as it likes to ogle Miss Mae West....North, east, south and west, not one motion-picture exhibitor has yet spurned a Mae West feature when it has been offered to him....Hundreds of Main Street theaters have booked her pictures for second engagements. In a few cases she has been called back for as many as seven repeats in one show-house."

Every few years the Motion Picture Producers and Distributors of America (MPPDA) had tried to establish a stronger hold over what actors could and couldn't say. The "Don'ts and Be Carefuls" list that Hays had decreed in 1927 had been merely an internal set of guidelines aimed at the studios' story departments. This sort of honor system gave way to a new code that was handed down in 1930 by a Jesuit priest, Father Daniel Lord, in consultation with Martin Quigley, an influential film-industry trade publisher. Under the new code, the Hays Office could order any number of deletions. When Warner gave Joan Blondell the script for *Convention City*, a 1933 movie in which she played the leading digger, she thought it was one of the funniest things ever written. But Dr. James Wingate, then head of MPPDA's "studio relations" committee, said that a line about "there ain't no Ten Commandments" could only pass if it was delivered without comic timing. Among the Wingate-inspired edits were the "indecent action" of Joan's lips in one scene, and this piece of dialogue: "Madame, I want my trousers." "You can have 'em if you come into the other room and take 'em off me!" But the code still depended on producers to police themselves, and it was obviously much weaker than Mae West, in spite of her concession to the "classy burglar" line.

Her other alternatives might have been, "You mean you turned her into a parasite?" Or "a gold digger." The muscle of various state censorship bodies had already placed a taboo on a long list of words and phrases, including "bitch," "chippy," "mistress," "harlot," "naked," "prostitute," "it wasn't love," and "you were with him all last night." Typical state restrictions decreed that a kiss could not last more than four feet of film, no woman or man could appear partly clad in the presence of the opposite sex, and a man could not slap a woman's posterior. But that wasn't enough.

The muscle of Quigley and Lord, along with state boards, had put a clamp on a "blue" version of Harlow's *Red Dust*, which circulated in naughty Europe. In 1934, the U.S. Marshal's office seized the circulating

Convention City
This travelling salesman comedy told about a convention of
the Honeywell Rubber Co. When Adolphe Menjou catches
the president going into a brothel, he is assured of a
promotion. Here he slips Joan Blondell her "fee."

91

copies of a Czechoslovakian import called *Ecstasy*, a dream-like tale of sensuous young wife/bald old husband/beefy young lover in which the curvy young brunette star, Hedwig Kiesler, was shown in a sensuous skinny dip. When she came to American soil and signed with MGM, the country knew her as that European "porn" star—so MGM cleared her name by changing it, to Hedy Lamarr.

The Hays Office already had an eagle eye on the murky goings-on in William Faulkner's perverse-sided South, but his novel *Sanctuary*, the story of pure southern womanhood turned on its ear and held willing prisoner in a bordello, had made it to the screen in 1933—with a few major facelifts. Faulkner himself had been inspired by the southern yellow press's shocker story of a criminal who had raped a young woman with a pistol, so Paramount made the picture with the claim that "social problems sanction art" as defense against the hand of Hays. It became *The Story of Temple Drake*, with Miriam Hopkins as the highborn southern belle who is raped by a gangster and abducted to a sinister house in Memphis. This was

tame compared to the novel: Faulkner had made Popeye an impotent thug who rapes Temple with a corncob. Then there was the

matter of the whorehouse. Whose idea was it to post a menu for soup and sandwiches, complete with cafeteria hours, on those tainted walls?

Nevertheless, the suppressed desires of Temple Drake gave taskmaster Hays more than one sleepless night. The studios faced the constant threat of economic ruin because the call to boycott unwholesome movies was resounding louder. Hays's job now was to ensure their survival—the most daunting task he had faced in this office, even more threatening than recent revelations about his own peccadilloes. Somehow, Hays had escaped scandal in 1928, when the word was out that, as chairman of the Republican National Committee, he had accepted a

BELOW: *The Story of Temple Drake*
"Don't bring your children to see this picture," proclaimed the ads for this film based on the book by William Faulkner. Star Miriam Hopkins said, "*Sanctuary* was done with fabulous style."

RIGHT: *Sanctuary*
Lee Remick stars as the southern bad girl in this adaptation of Faulkner's novel. When Hedda Hopper asked about playing the bad girl role, Ms. Remick replied, "They seem to feel I carry these roles around with me; but to me its just acting."

OPPOSITE: *The Strange Woman*
Star Hedy Lamarr said of her producing debut: "It's wonderful to be associated with people who listen to my ideas."

$75,000 "gift" and a $185,000 "loan" from Harry Sinclair of the Teapot Dome scandals, gratitude money for his behind-the-scenes efforts at pushing Warren G. Harding into the White House. In 1930, he had been caught paying bribe money of his own to civic and religious leaders who were supposed to render unbiased judgments on the cleanliness of films. Furthermore, his efforts to court the press, playing public relations agent for all of Hollywood by inviting eastern writers out to show them what an upstanding, wholesome place sunny Lotus Land was, had not kept nasty tales from escaping. Studio hush money had been reasonably effective in putting a press gag on Clara Bow's visits to the abortionist and the VD clinic, but when a private detective exposed Dr. William Earl Pearson's personal therapy for her nerves and insomnia to Mrs. Pearson, who promptly sued Bow for alienation of affection, nothing could stop the tabloids. That story, combined with Daisy DeVoe's revelations, was Bow's undoing. Hays couldn't do a thing about the rumors that Mae West was really a man, or the steady stream of police reports on

95

unnamed starlets picked up for vagrancy or street trade. Most of them were unknowns, but every unemployed or working "professional" young lady in Hollywood claimed to be an actress by trade.

But that was only real life. What worried the entire MPPDA in 1934 was the new, improved Catholic anti-smut lobby, in the form of the Legion of Decency, whose

RIGHT: *The Big Heat*
Of the filming Gloria Grahame said, "I just remember Lee Marvin threw coffee, honey. It must have been cold, but I didn't think much about that. Whatever they told me to do, I did."

ABOVE: Many actresses wanted to be in *Gone with the Wind*, and when Ona Munson (the madam in *Shanghai Gesture*) auditioned, she wore four-inch platform heels to appear taller. Commenting on the character, she said, "I say Belle wasn't a hussy. There was nothing mean, petty or catty about her. I'll take up arms for Belle's character any old time. She was vital and warm and had the traditional 'heart of gold.'"

ABOVE: *Dr. Jekyll and Mr. Hyde*
Miriam Hopkins didn't want the part in this 1931 version, but the studio insisted. Later she commented on playing a bad woman: "I enjoyed playing that sort of woman. They have the courage of the damned. They know what they want and go right ahead."

OPPOSITE: *Dr. Jekyll and Mr. Hyde*
In an unusual turn of events, Ingrid Bergman asked to be cast as the bad woman in this 1941 version, and switched roles with Lana Turner who was happy to portray a good woman. Many felt that no one would take Ms. Bergman seriously as a bad woman. Lana Turner said, "Spencer wanted me to play both the bad and the good girls, but the studio wouldn't let him have his way."

members took an oath to condemn offensive films and not attend them. Priests across the country had their parishioners reciting the oath during Sunday mass.

The Hays Office responded with a new code with powers of enforcement. First they drew up a rigorous document of rules, which began by stating: "No picture shall be produced that will lower the moral standards of those who see it. The sympathy of the audience shall never be thrown to the side of crime, wrongdoing, evil or sin." Then they created the Production Code Administration (PCA), headed up by a young altar-boy-turned-newspaperman named Joseph Breen. Thereafter, when the Hays Office gave its approval to a movie, the PCA then gave it a seal of purity. The signatories to the code agreed that a film would not be distributed or exhibited without the PCA seal. The rule was highly enforceable since the MPPDA members were the very studios that owned nearly all of the cinemas in the country, and many abroad. Therefore, a film without the seal would be available only in back alleys.

The code wasn't enough to drive Mae West out of town, but it did put an end to her glory days. She still managed to slip some worthy West-isms into *Belle of the Nineties*, such as, "It is better to be looked over than overlooked," and "A man in the house is worth two in the street," but her old vaudeville gem, "Is that a gun in your pocket, or are you just glad to see me?" didn't make it. Nor did the original title of this fifth West feature remain unchanged—Paramount was all set to release the movie as *It Ain't No Sin*, but the title itself became a prime target for the Legionnaires of Decency.

The 1936 film *Klondike Annie* had Mae West playing a bawdy-house singer who flees to the Klondike to escape the law, disguising

herself in the clothes of a dead missionary. Looking deliciously ludicrous in a high-necked frock and bonnet, the bad woman begins to "see things different." A formula by which a bad girl movie could get the PCA seal of purity was evolving, and the producers were trying to "pass" by making films wherein the bad woman is reformed, killed, or punished by the end of the movie. "Annie" decided to face justice and accept her punishment.

Jean Harlow's hair became darker in her 1936 movie, *Wife Versus Secretary*, and all she got to do with Clark Gable was take his shoes off. Joe Breen got huffy about the size of her apartment in this movie. Keep it small, he decreed, or else it will look as though she's augmenting her secretarial salary with other

favors. Ornate residences, large diamonds, and white telephones—the French kind, beside the bed, that seemed like vintage Harlow after she used one to coo with her personal physician in *Dinner at Eight*—were dead giveaways of an unfettered lady. (In Italy, there is still a genre known as " white telephone" movies.)

As the Code War waged on, harlotry became the stuff of heavy-handed dramas. Some were good, some were trite, and some are classifiable as high camp today because they were oh-so seriously moralistic in their time. But none let the bad girls have much fun. The new "personality" actresses, the ones who could pause drolly and deliver crackling repartee, were Rosalind Russell, Katharine Hepburn, Carole Lombard, and Myrna Loy, who were at their best as "screwball" society wits and plucky, unstoppable career women. The heavyweight leading ladies—Crawford, Bette Davis, Vivien Leigh, Ingrid Bergman, Barbara Stanwyck—managed to avoid becoming stereotyped, and played themselves playing whatever role the occasion demanded. When Bergman decided it was time American audiences see her versatility, she asked if she could switch roles with Lana Turner in the

1941 version of *Dr. Jekyll and Mr. Hyde*, with Spencer Tracy turning into hairy Hyde. Bergman had been cast as Dr. Jekyll's snowy pure fiancée, but instead she played the cockney strumpet who is punished for her low birth when Mr. Hyde beats her to death.

Turner, of course, was one of the assembly line blondes, fashioned from an elegant mold that Ginger Rogers pioneered when she shed her cherubic cheeks and exchanged the coin costume for ballroom couture. The cool, svelte beauties who were typically called upon to play the woman with a past were more or less interchangeable. Tay Garnett, the director who changed Joan Bennett from blonde to brunette in 1939's *Trade Winds*—and as an unexpected bonus, altered her "type" from innocent ingenue to nouvelle vamp—pointed out that, "She looks like a blonde Hedy Lamarr anyway." Ann Sheridan, who was called The "Oooomph" Girl to replace and recycle The "It" Girl, looked like a brown-haired Lana Turner. "Ooomph"—derived from the sound a fat man makes when he squeezes out of a phone booth—was minus the bounce and fizz of "It." As Lola of the "juke joints" in *Juke Girl* (a Code-ese term for a B-girl), hired to mingle with male customers, hustle them for drinks before closing time, and then provide intimate favors afterward, she played her by-then-typical tough, cynical role. She sang "I Hates Love But I Loves to Hate It" in a way that said not even love will put life into this bad girl, though it was a song that Dietrich could have turned into a three-ring orgy. Sheridan's leading man, however, gave an almost-convincing performance of a down-and-out Depression era drifter engaged in a heroic effort to defend the farmers of Florida. The "aw shucks" kind of guy who thought he should forgive the juke girl's past because "I

TOP: *South Sea Woman*
Virginia Mayo is a camera girl in the Pink Lotus nightclub in Shanghai. She said the movie was "so romantic it would be a real handholder."

BOTTOM: *Juke Girl*
This melodrama was shot in Cat Tail, Florida. Advertisements proclaimed: "She makes her living the hard way, the five cents a dance way. But don't get ideas, buddy, she's a one man woman and that man ain't you" and "I don't care what women think of me as long as men think of me. I am easy to meet but hard to forget." The studio advised the exhibitors to promote juke boxes in their lobbies.

Rancho Notorious
In order to discover the murderer of his bride, the groom winds up at the Chuck-a-Luck Ranch run by Altar Keane, the bandit queen. This is a flashback scene, during which a cowboy says, "I remember how it used to be...." Marlene was very unhappy with her look in this film. The director, Fritz Lang, said, "Driving home one night I saw a light on up on the fourth floor in the studio building. I was astonished at what I saw: Marlene was standing there taking photos of herself in a mirror with flashbulbs, testing herself for the next day's work."

still think you're okay," was a lean, young bumpkin type named Ronald Reagan.

Playing Slut Scrabble, inventing euphemisms for The Word in Code dialect, became the only way to make a movie about a bad woman, but even the profession had to be thinly veiled. Ronnie Reagan's love interest called herself "a juke joint sister," and that passed the PCA. When Claudette Colbert starred in *Zaza* (1939), a tale of a Parisian dance hall wench who loves a married man but gives him up when she finds out he has a wife, *Zaza* could have been Little Mary

Sunshine of the cabarets except for a one-line indictment: "I saw him leaving the theatre with a woman. She asked him to take her out for a cup of chocolate. That's what respectable women drink late at night, you know."

But the ads could promise what the picture couldn't deliver.

Claimed an ad for newly dark-tressed Joan Bennett's 1939 movie, *The Housekeeper's Daughter*, in which she played a young coquette whose mother runs a boarding house patronized by thieves, murderers, mayhem, and reporters:

"She couldn't cook and
She couldn't sew,
But, oh, how she
Could so-and-so."

Joan protested to the Hays Office, but Hays replied that he had no control over the advertising, only the picture.

The setting for a picture was another giveaway: if the cameras panned across an Old West desert, a breezy South Sea island, or the streets of Old Shanghai, it was a pretty safe bet that a woman engaged in the unmentionable trade would show up, looking nothing like the kind of girl who might live next door. As Gaby in *Algiers*, Hedy Lamarr, with diamonds gleaming against the exotic music of the Casbah, gave her profession away only by the presence of a portly old man—and one line. When she's planning to run off with the smitten thief Pepe Le Moko (Charles Boyer), who's willing to risk arrest by the French gendarmes to flee the Casbah with her, she tells her rich provider that he can't stop her from becoming to Pepe Le Moko "the same thing I am to you."

And who was really fooled at the sight of Lute Mae's "Road House" in *Flamingo Road*, with La Crawford as the "waitress" in the exotic land of redneck sheriffs and Faulkneristic schemers? Dietrich's best pictures had seen their day by then, but *The Flame of New Orleans* had an amusing nondescription of the gold-digging woman of the world she played: "What a girl! What stories!...They say she used to fake fainting spells."

"What a witches' sabbath... so incredibly evil. I didn't think such a place existed except in my own imagination—like a half-remembered dream. Anything could happen here, at any moment," said a tipsy-looking Gene Tierney in Von Sternberg's baroque and ominous *Shanghai Gesture*. The evil place is a gambling den, and the gaming table has bewitched Poppy(Gene Tierney), as has the opiate that her name suggests. That much is visible. The audience even learns the truth about the sinister proprietor named Mother Gin Sling (Ona Munson), who gets Poppy hooked so that she'll run up a heavy debt, which will place some obligations upon Poppy's father, British financier Sir Guy Charteris, who has put the local authorities under pressure to close Mother Gin Sling's den. It's Poppy's own mother who is using her this way. Only Mother knows that Charteris is the man she married years before, the man who thought his Shanghai wife had been murdered and fled with her estate and their infant daughter. Mother loses control and shoots Poppy at the end of the movie. And this was the whitewashed version; the Hays Office had rejected nearly three dozen earlier film treatments of the popular 1925 play set in Mother Goddam's brothel. "Change her name!" ordered Hays when he finally capitulated. The true nature of Gin Sling's establishment unfolds in "quickie" scenes. Early on she purchases a blonde named Dixie from the police, and on New Year's Eve she

auctions women who are suspended in cages.

The true nature of Claire Trevor's occupation in John Ford's Wild West epic, *Stagecoach*, is revealed by the fact that the Ladies' Law and Order League escorts her to the stagecoach, ordering her out of town, and the way her fellow passengers, especially the pregnant married lady, shun her. Dallas marries outlaw-with-a-heart John Wayne for redemption, but when Magnificent Marlene took Lola Lola out west, in *Destry Rides Again*, and later in *Rancho Notorious*, she became the kind of saloon girl every outlaw needs—a woman who'll sashay in front of a bullet to save the man she loves. Another death in *Destry* was that of a scene in which a cowpoke looks down Marlene's low-cut *bustier* and says, "Thar's gold in them thar hills!" The line disappeared after the sneak preview.

That old staple from the Prohibition Age, the gangster's moll, came back many times in a new wave of mob mania. But the old urban outlaw-hero who brought a little bootleg cheer into American lives became a cold-blooded killer under the Code, which happened to come along about the same time as Repeal. Jimmy Cagney was a tough guy with guts (the male equivalent of a P with an H of G) in *The Public Enemy* in 1931—no matter that the movie is best remembered for

---

ABOVE LEFT: *Maltese Falcon*
To prepare for the "I'm a liar, I've always been a liar" scene, Mary Astor reported that, "I hyperventilated before going into most of the scenes." After receiving an Oscar for *The Great Lie* in the same year, she commented, "If I had my druthers, I would have preferred getting my Oscar for Brigid."

ABOVE RIGHT: *Dead End*
Claire Trevor was called the "Queen of the B's." When she tells Humphrey Bogart that she resorted to prostitution while he was away (in jail), he responds: "Why didn't you starve?" Director William Wyler told her the day before the scene was shot: "When you get up in the morning, don't comb your hair, come to the studio exactly as you get out of bed." She said, "It only took a day and one half to shoot and I was so disappointed."

OPPOSITE: *Key Largo*
Claire Trevor plays an alcoholic mistress of a gangster. Here she's being threatened by one of his henchmen. Claire Trevor commented that, "if a part has enough facets, I don't mind playing the bad girl."

The Monster and the Girl
She's captured by a white slave ring. Her brother attempts to rescue her and he's magically transformed into a gorilla by a mad scientist in this spoof of the white slave genre.

the scene in which he mashes a grapefruit in
Mae Clarke's face. But the very next year, the
mobsters of America began to show a
particularly mean streak. The Lindbergh baby
kidnapping was one nasty episode—and
shortly after, Marlene Dietrich received some
anonymous letters threatening to kidnap her
daughter. By the time Humphrey Bogart
played the legendary killer Baby Face Martin
in *Dead End* (1937), the gangster had lost all
redeeming virtues—except, perhaps, the
capacity to love, mobster style."Why didn't
you starve first?" asks an unforgiving Bogey of
his burned out, "sick" (with a disease that was
also unmentionable) ex-girlfriend Francie,
played by Claire Trevor.

That same year, in *Marked Woman*, Bogey
played one of his rare good-guy roles as
district attorney David Graham, and cracked
the Club Intime, a "clip joint" that seemed
strangely reminiscent of a kind of house oft-
featured in a kind of movie that could no
longer be made. Since the Code stated clearly:
"White slavery shall not be treated," Bette
Davis and her four "roommates" became
hostesses who couldn't escape their racketeer
boss. Since the movie was based on the life
story of Lucky Luciano, a white slaver among
other things, and Bogart's character on
Thomas E. Dewey, who prosecuted Luciano,
Bette's profession became "unsavory and
distasteful," as Graham put it in court. "The
truth is that these women, in the face of sheer,
stark terrorism, did appear in court, expose
themselves to public gaze, told the truth
about themselves, told the world what they
really are," he summed up. What were they?
The audience was left to fill in the blank
space.

"What is your occupation?," another
attorney asks another distressed young *fille de
joie*, named Susan, played by Ellen Drew, in

the campiest disguised-white-slavery movie ever, *The Monster and the Girl*, made in 1940. The girl just hangs her head. The jury murmurs. So much for her testimony, which happens to be in defense of her brother, on trial for murdering a man in the white slave racket. Thanks to her unnamed occupation, justice is not served until her brother agrees to bide his prison term by participating in a scientist's laboratory experiment, and comes back as a hairy ape. Poor Susan did not notice that when she "married" the friendly but shifty-eyed Larry Reed, the "minister" had a gun protruding from his hip pocket.

Cracking the classics was another challenge for the studios. Samuel Goldwyn was keeping a Russian blonde in his private life who had the perfect face and accent—in his mind—to be groomed for Garbo-hood. Instead of becoming Garbo II, however, Anna Sten went

down in history as Goldwyn's Edsel. Her acting was no worse than that of many others from the stable of classic pretties, but she just didn't click. But as Nana, a courtesan *fatale* who devoured the men of Paris in Emile Zola's novel, Sten did receive an Honorary Heart of Gold, courtesy of Will Hays. Nana of the novel believed that men were strictly for bestowing mother-of-pearl-handled fans and solid gold beds and she died wretchedly, of smallpox, looking "as though the poison she had assimilated in the gutters...had but now remounted to her face." This kind of punishment seemed a tad unphotogenic, however, so Nana, though called by one spurned lover a "gilded fly, that's hatched in the gutter, that carries poison," dies of a sudden attack of nobility. As two brothers prepare to duel over her, a shot is heard from the sanctum where she plies her trade. "I can't separate brothers," breathes the dying Nana, as the bullet pierces her chest.

Forever Amber, starring Linda Darnell and based on Kathleen Winsor's book on the life of Amber St. Clare, mistress to Charles II, was one of the four top-grossing pictures of 1947, but Amber had to lose any number of husbands and lovers to get a PCA seal. From Restoration records, author Winsor had uncovered four husbands, three or four children, and a galaxy of lovers who paved

LEFT: *Nana*
Anna Sten's accent was so thick that she could not pronounce Nana, and it came out Anna. When she was learning to dance, Sam Goldwyn jumped around the floor on one foot to show her that even a middle-aged man could can-can. He finally hired Dorothy Arzner to direct, who stated: "I sort of salvaged the thing, but I wish the script were stronger."

OPPOSITE: *Nana*
Martine Carroll was called the Marilyn Monroe of France. She commented: "We have changed the story around: I get strangled in the end."

Amber's path from tavern wench to the King's palace. On the screen she married only once, had one child, and a paltry four lovers. Though the book ended with Amber departing for America, still out to snag her roving lover Bruce Carlton (Cornel Wilde), the movie went for the redemption option. Bruce, determined to lead a clean life, absolved himself of Amber, and a sniffling Amber headed back to a simple life with a palace handyman.

As Allied and Axis powers readied for combat, was it espionage for art's sake that led to the shocking reports that the Princess Pola Negri, at large in Europe again, was conducting private negotiations with Adolph Hitler. If there was actually a Nazi in her life, though, it was more likely to be Goebbels, who was the Third Reich's Minister of Culture, and was known to have met with her in his office when she called as emissary for the German film industry, with a plea for freedom of expression.

Whatever really went on in those secret chambers, the idea of bedding a bad girl with the enemy seemed irresistible in wartime scripts. The Unspeakable Profession found its way to World War II in a string of movies featuring leading ladies practicing counterespionage with their lipstick on. The most memorable of the honorable women in dishonorable service was Ingrid Bergman as a party girl called upon to serve her adopted country in the early postwar Hitchcock

Forever Amber
The film was adapted from the novel, but the censor stipulated there were to be no bathing or bedroom scenes. In the casting stages of the film, Preminger wanted Lana Turner and told Darryl Zanuck who said, "Why should we pay MGM, we could use our Linda Darnell." So he arranged an informal dinner party and Lana practically climbed into Darryl's lap.

thriller *Notorious*. Seducing, then marrying, a loathsome Nazi to find his secret mines seemed an appropriate atonement for her past sins, and as luck would have it, Cary Grant rescued her at the end to complete her redemption.

Was it an attempt to strive for the grit of realism that gave rise to the gloomy thrillers that came to be known as film noir? Fritz Lang has claimed he started out just wanting to present a sympathetic portrait of a working girl when he directed Joan Bennett in *Man Hunt*, released in 1941, the first of the famous Lang/Bennett Bleak Trilogy. For Joan it was a great escape from what she called "all that blonde bland innocence" of her earlier career. And for Hays it was another heavy cutting job. As a martyred cockney waif who plies her trade for Gestapo agents, in order to throw them off the track of the English big-game hunter she loves, Joan was ordered to be careful not to swing her purse back and forth while walking the streets. And then Lang had a brainstorm for getting around the Code. He called the props department and got a sewing machine for her apartment, so that she could be a seamstress for all practical purposes.

The seamstress paraphernalia came in handy for their next film together, *The Woman in the Window*, in which she played an artist's model who dupes Edward G. Robinson, playing a psychology professor, and she ends up getting stabbed with a pair of scissors. In *Scarlet Street*, based on the heavy handed French picture, Jean Renoir's *La Chienne* (The Bitch), itself based on the play by George de la Foucharchère, Bennett was a strumpet pure and simple, out to ruin Robinson, in the role of an unhappy henpecked cashier who dreams of being a famous painter. This time Robinson stabs her with an ice pick, but Hays asked Lang to lighten up on the punishment, and cut the number of stabs from seven to one.

Five years later, Bennett's husband, Walter Wanger, brought a little realité noir into their lives. Bennett had been spending a bit too much time "doing" the Hollywood night life with her agent, Jennings Lang, and Wanger already had private detectives on her tail. On December 13, 1951, as Bennett was returning from an ostensible "business lunch" with Lang, Wanger surprised them in the parking lot outside Lang's office. He fired two shots. One went wild, the other richocheted off the ground and hit Lang in the groin. He recovered, and Wanger spent 101 days at the Wayside Honor Farm in Castaic, California, before he went to work at Allied Artists, but Bennett's career was never the same. "I became a professional outcast. Everybody sort of thought I was taboo," she told an interviewer later.

Some facts of life even the Code couldn't hide. A shocked America learned that Ingrid Bergman was pregnant by her director, Roberto Rossellini, when she was filming *Stromboli* in 1949—and furthermore, she had no plans to marry him. But when she took off for Europe with her infant son to escape the wagging tongues, she soon found she wasn't the only Hollywoodite in temporary exile

Woman in the Window and *Scarlet Street*
Both movies were very similar in theme—except that Joan Bennett gets killed by scissors in *The Woman in the Window* and by an ice pick in *Scarlet Street*. Edward G. Robinson said, "I have nothing against Joan Bennett, but if the script mentions that she must die, die she must." Explaining that the theme bothered him, he commented, "The first time was during the filming of *Woman in the Window* and I almost got her that time, the police got me first. Now I don't have a chance and I'm getting rather angry. I should win Joan, it is one of the aims of my life."

The Great Stars and Director of "Woman in the Window"....

WALTER WANGER presents

a FRITZ LANG Production

EDWARD G. ROBINSON   JOAN BENNETT

Scarlet Street

with DAN DURYEA

The things she
does to men
can only end
in Murder!

"Hello, Lazylegs..."

A DIANA PRODUCTION
Produced and Directed by
FRITZ LANG
A UNIVERSAL RELEASE

JESS BARKER · MARGARET LINDSAY · ROSALIND IVAN · SAMUEL S. HINDS
Based on the novel "La Chienne"   Screenplay by DUDLEY NICHOLS   Art Direction by Alexander Golitzen

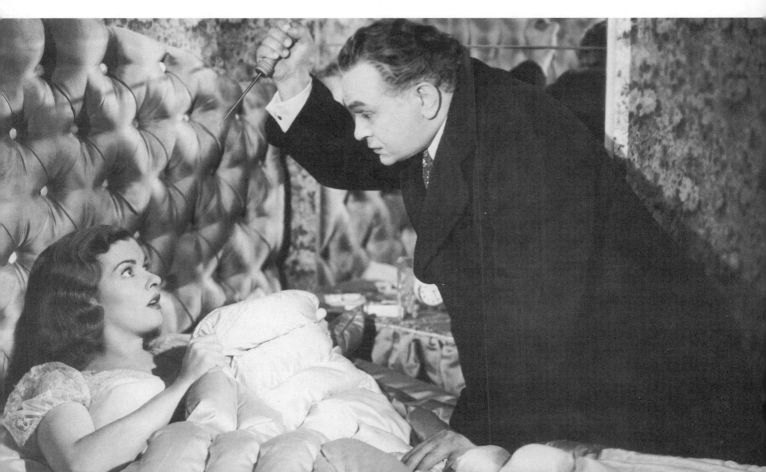

there. The 1951 raid of Madam Billy Bennett's pleasure palace in the Hollywood Hills sent many famous male customers scurrying around the world, waiting for the studios to hush the law and the press. All of Billy's clientele had signed her guest book. Some had left their Oscars on her mantel as mementoes. The Czar of Virtue had no comment; real life was out of his control.

ABOVE: *Razor's Edge*
Anne Baxter goes from nice girl to Parisian slut. Here she's overcome by a drug-induced drunken stupor. She recalls, "I knew about the film....It never occurred to me that they'd even consider me for the part."

RIGHT: *Razor's Edge*
A remake of the 1946 classic, this version stars Theresa Russell and Bill Murray.

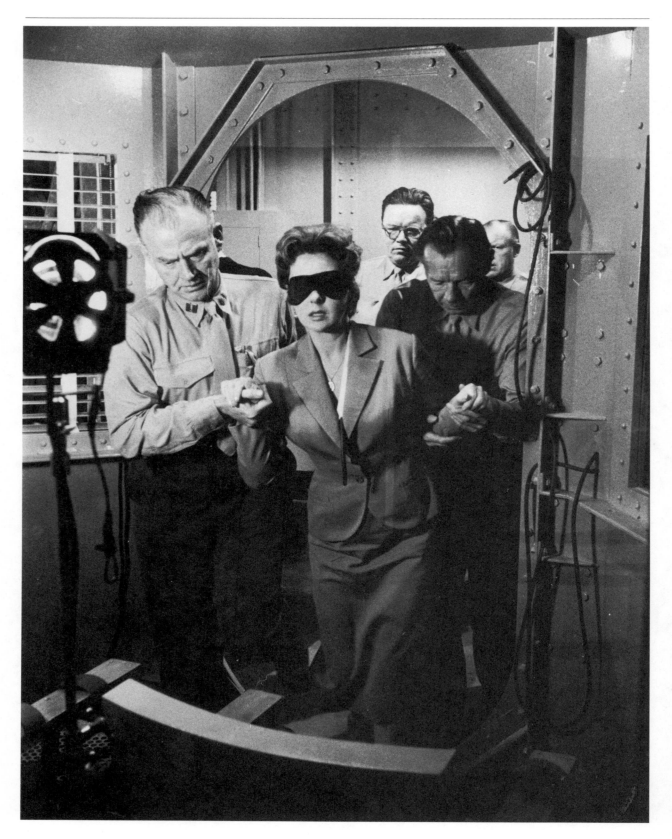

THE BAD WIFE

A woman accused of having fatally stabbed her husband while her two children watched was charged yesterday with homicide while she was in a hospital in critical condition from an overdose of sleeping pills.

The patient was Mrs. Camilla Failla, 32 years old, of 72 Lamport Place, the Bronx. The police said she had killed her 38-year-old husband, Joseph, after an argument about letters from a woman she had found in his pocket [sic].

The crime was discovered by the police after they had been called to the Failla home by a 10-year-old daughter of the couple. The girl and her 8-year-old brother were

questioned after the girl told the police her mother had stabbed her father, according to the police.

When the police reached the house, Mr. Failla, who is part owner of two dress factories, was still alive, bleeding from thirteen wounds. . . .

In checking on the stories the police found in the living room of the Failla home, at the base of the Christmas tree, a mink coat valued at $5,000 that Mr. Failla had given his wife for Christmas. . . .*

The estate of Joseph R. Failla, 39-year-old [sic] Bronx manufacturer who was stabbed to death in his home on Christmas morning, was left to his widow, Camilla, 32, who is charged with killing him, it was disclosed yesterday in Bronx Surrogates Court. . . .The value of the estate was said to be $100,000.†

Mrs. Camilla Failla, 32-year-old mother of two children, who stabbed and killed her husband, Joseph, 38, on Chirstmas morning in their home at 72 Lamport Place, the Bronx, was committed yesterday by Bronx County Judge Harry Stackell to Rockland State Hospital.

Mrs. Failla pleaded guilty to a first degree murder indictment with a specification of

---

I Want to Live
This is the story of Barbara Graham, an ex-prostitute who tried to reform, and the first woman in California to be sentenced to the death penalty. All the way to the gas chamber Barbara, portrayed by Susan Hayward, told the authorities that she'd been home with her husband and son the night of the murder. Unfortunately her junkie husband had skipped out on her and could not be reached for comment. In the final scenes, on her way to her death, she sadly repeats, "My Henry was a wonderful husband...I had an ideal marriage."

---

*The New York Times, December 26, 1949, page 13.
†The New York Times, January 8, 1950 page 58.
§The New York Times, January 31, 1950 page 29.

insanity. Psychiatrists at Bellevue Hospital reported that she was insane and should be committed to Matteawan State Hospital. Her attorney pleaded with the court to send her to Rockland State Hospital because a cure could be effected more quickly there. If Mrs. Failla is released from the hospital she will face the murder indictment.

Before committing Mrs. Failla, Judge Stackell said: "This case is a tragedy, a very sad and unfortunate occurrence. The probation report showed that her husband was devoted and loving, both as a father and husband. He left his entire estate to her."§

Judging by the fact that she attacked her husband in the heat of an argument, with her children present through the whole sordid affair, Camilla Failla does sound unstable. If her motivation had been to get her hands on the $100,000 estate, she could have been more calculating. (As it happened, she never lived to see a penny—she committed suicide while still under psychiatric observation.) But on the other hand, assuming that she married for love more than 10 years earlier, and had grown to feel like a drab *hausfrau* at the age of 32, with a husband who mollified her with

OPPOSITE: *Madame X*
Pauline Frederick played this role on the stage and also in a film version in 1920. On opening night in New York, 14,000 people attended. She used hardly any make-up except for deep shadows under her eyes and gray streaks in her hair. Discussing the role, she said she loved "letting it up with the old rips!"

TOP LEFT: *Madame X*
Gladys George appeared in the road company performance by Pauline Frederick in her 1921–1925 tour as did unknown actor Clark Cable. In 1937 she portrayed Madame X and said "I don't care if I look 16 to 60 behind the lights if only the role permits me to create a character that is entertaining."

MIDDLE LEFT: *Madame X*
Ruth Chatterton, a stage actress, portrayed Madame X on the screen in 1929. This type of story was referred to by many actresses as one of those "16 to 60" things and she stated, "I always wonder why an actress wants to hold on and play young parts. There's nothing interesting about a girl in a white dress and a blue sash. The greatest success has been made in heavy roles." Quite the adventuress, she flew her own plane from Los Angeles to New York and sponsored the Ruth Chatterton Air Derby.

BOTTOM LEFT: *Madame X*
Lana Turner suggested to Ross Hunter, the producer of the 1966 version that she portray Madame X and saw the first two remakes, but the Gladys George version convinced her to do it. A scheming mother in-law is added to this final film version. It was elaborately mounted with $87,000 worth of furs and clothes.

mink coats while his affections wandered to more provocative women, she would have had little outlet for expressing her hurt and rage in 1949. Anyone she turned to—family, friends, clergymen, lawyers, psychoanalysts—would have probably told her that a wife must work hard to reignite her husband's interest when he becomes bored. Divorce was considered "failure to adjust"—at least if you were the ordinary wife of an ordinary garment manufacturer.

If she ever leafed through Hollywood fan magazines, Mrs. Failla would have been well aware that movie stars lived by a different set of mating rules. By 1949 Rita Hayworth had divorced her husband/pimp Ed Judson on a charge of cruelty and polished her GI pinup goddess image by marrying Orson Welles—considered the most cerebral inhabitant of Hollywood—only to shed him after four turbulent years. Lana Turner, the miner's daughter who rose from white-trash shantyville to stardom, had already bedded with gangsters and hoped in vain for a proposal from Howard Hughes, and was on her third husband—this one a millionaire who had soothed her broken heart when Tyrone Power dumped her. But for Mrs. Failla, and hundreds of thousands of other American housewives, Rita Hayworth and Lana Turner were something other than real people. They wore sequined lamé gowns and had perfect curves—no flesh-and-blood mortal ever looked like that. Movie stars were celestial beings, who, for all anyone in the Bronx or Levittown knew, didn't even have the same internal organs as real people. Whatever cosmic force made them creatures without flab, clogged pores, bad breath, *or* household chores also absolved them from ordinary obligations to sweat it out in a marriage that was anything less than perpetual romantic bliss. People who were *that* beautiful were expected to live idyllic, trouble-free lives.

So, because a star was supposed to smile, around the same time Camilla Failla was schlepping her baby daughter's carriage around the neighborhood, Margarita Carmen Cansino was acting almost every night. She was playing the role of a radiantly happy young starlet who was madly in love with the much older man who was squiring her to every movie premiere in Hollywood and thrusting her upon every photographer and gossip columnist in the vicinity. Ed Judson,

who was about the same age as Margarita's father, had made his fortune as a promoter of foreign cars, and had decided to turn his talents to peddling the daughter of the famous dancing Cansinos. She struck out in a series of unmemorable films before Judson, claiming the title of agent, talked Harry Cohn into giving her a chance. Margarita's instructions from her husband/agent were simple: "be nice" to Cohn. Judson showed his bride off in lamé gowns, and made sure her name got into newspaper columns. But even when Harry Cohn turned out to be wild about her, Judson perceived that Margarita needed a few more touches. At last it came to him. He had her black hair dyed red, and put her through an excrutiating year-long series of electrolysis treatments on her hairline so that she would emerge with a breathtaking brow. And then he changed her name to Rita Hayworth.

Fans were not shocked when the Judson-Hayworth divorce proceedings took a nasty turn, because what man wouldn't put up a fight if Rita Hayworth were dumping him? It seemed absolutely gallant of Harry Cohn to come through with the $30,000 in damages that Judson had demanded from Hayworth as payment in kind for all he had done for her. If the studio magnate was in love with the star, that was okay too—what man wasn't in love with Rita Hayworth? Because she was a star, she was not expected to be a good, domestic wife.

In 1947, while Hayworth was divorcing her second spouse, the women in Camilla Failla's circle were reading the bestselling *Modern Woman: The Lost Sex*, by psychoanalyst Marynia Farnham and sociologist Ferdinand Lundberg, and learning the definition of true womanhood: "self-acceptance, dependence on men, and passive fulfillment in sex and

ABOVE: *I Cover the Waterfront*
Claudette Colbert confronts her father at a bordello and deals with business on his behalf with the Madam. She's explaining that it's fine that he pays money for services, but he shouldn`t be robbed of all his money.

LEFT: *East of Eden*
Jo Van Fleet won an Academy Award for best actress. She explained, "I did receive a lot of letters asking me to tell about James Dean. They seem to feel that he should have won the Oscar." John Steinbeck wrote the book and stated, "I'm glad my book has contributed...to what is probably the best motion picture I have ever seen."

121

2009-127

122

motherhood." The media were telling them about the great pleasures to be discovered in jaunts to such accessible destinations as the kitchen. A 1947 ad from the National Dairy Products Corporation proclaimed beneath a picture of a beaming young wife in a housedress and apron watching her beaming husband examine the pot on the stove, "Prediction: the new wives of 1947 are going to have more fun in the kitchen. Previous cooking experience is desirable, perhaps, but not essential. There are so many new easy-to-use foods, so many new ways to prepare foods, so many interesting ways to serve foods, cooking will be a novel and exciting adventure."

A bad wife in the postwar era would, naturally, be likely to search for adventures outside the kitchen—and possibly even yearn for lamé and flashbulbs. The anti-Hollywood Hollywood movie didn't spring up *just* to aid the unofficial Scurry-to-the-Kitchen Movement, but any mid-American housewife with Beverly Hills on the brain could see her fantasies quickly dashed by such movies as *The Big Knife*, in which Jack Palance played Charlie Castle, an actor who has sold his soul to be top box-office material, embroiled in scandal and unable to restore domestic bliss with Marion, the wife he loves, played by Ida Lupino. "Stop trying to be a housewife," he tells her when she attempts to pick up his highball, and from the longing gaze in her eyes, it's evident that Marion would rather be in a tiny tract home anywhere but where she

is. But the anti-Hollywood movie only incidentally told the suburban masses that their lives were enviable—the genre's real purpose being the in-house intelligentsia's reaction to the abominations of McCarthyism and to Will Hays's cornball efforts to hype Tinseltown as a fine and proper place. The nationwide effort to send Rosie the Riveter back to the kitchen so that returning veterans could have their jobs back and American nuclear families of all classes could show the dirty Reds that democracy meant prosperous, homespun bliss, was, of course, captured for posterity by domestic sitcoms that could be seen in wholesome family togetherness on the new American shrine, the television set. This medium of clean family entertainment showed how a wife should behave—while the movies were able to employ the well-trod formula by which bad people could be bad to the core as long as they were reformed, killed, or punished within the space of two hours, to illustrate everything a wife should *not* be.

The Big Lesson was, simply, don't marry for money. In an earlier, more decadent age, Wallace Beery had loved letting Jean Harlow plunder his pockets, and Aline MacMahon had found a pompous, yet lovable rich old coot in cherub-faced Guy Kibbee. But as suburbia blossomed and more 19-year-old women than ever before had babies, gold digging became strictly *verboten*. Only one element of the sport remained intact: the woman who panned for gold was brassy and cheap, given to wearing ensembles with too little fabric and too many accessories, ascending from a place where men called her a "dame" and were frequently out of work. Even marriage could never fully absolve That Kind of Woman from her roots. She was too clearly a woman who had managed to wangle a license to be kept.

Double Indemnity
Barbara Stanwyck explained her initial reaction to Billy Wilder, "I was scared because I'd never before played an out-and-out killer. I was scared...and I thought this role was gonna finish me." He cajoled her into accepting by asking: "Are you an actress or a mouse?"

Throughout the ages, many experts have argued that prostitution is not strictly an economically based institution. In 1937, sociologist Kingsley Davis wrote that a prostitute's financial return "is primarily a reward for loss of social standing. She loses social esteem because our moral system condemns the commercialization of intercourse." He believed it was incorrect to define prostitution simply as the use of sexual responses for an ulterior purpose because "this would include a great portion of all social behavior, especially that of women. It would include marriage, for example, wherein women trade their sexual favors for an economic and social status supplied by men." The cinematic gold digger, however, accepted money, diamonds, penthouses, and even the title of "Mrs." in return for a social ostracism that she would never, in a million years, be able to live down.

Though there were, in reality, more rich men to go around than there had been in the reign of Harlow, West, and the other master "diggers," the Bad Wife of the affluent postwar age had a propensity for picking the meanest sugar daddy in town. If she turned out to be a femme fatale who married, then enticed some virile young pauper to help her kill her mate for his money and her freedom, she could hardly be blamed. Director Billy

LEFT: *The Postman Always Rings Twice*
The story was bought in 1935 and people anxiously awaited for the film to be released, as the novel was so popular and steamy. The director commented that "It was a real chore to do the film under The Breen Office. . .." On the set John Garfield yelled out "Hey Lana, how about a quickie," to the crew's amusement. Lana Turner who called herself the "Queen of the Worrywarts," said that, "John Garfield had a terrific magnetism. The lines just bounced back and forth between us."

ABOVE: *The Sin of Madelon Claudet*
Helen Hayes's husband Charles MacArthur worked on the
script and said, "Helen got an Oscar for the sin of Madelon
Claudet and all I got was a brain tumor." It's roughly the same
story as *Madame X*.

RIGHT: *Clash by Night*
Director Fritz Lang commented, "I did a lot of research about
the faithfulness of wives and I found in one of the leading
magazines that 75% of all married women have betrayed their
husbands."

126

Wilder and screenwriter Raymond Chandler set up the morbid genre in 1944 with *Double Indemnity*, based on James M. Cain's novella, with Barbara Stanwyck as Phyllis Dietrichson, the tawdry, taunting, blonde, over-lipsticked wife of a man who made her flesh crawl. By the same token, the situation could lead to an automatic deduction that a gold-digging wife was also an adulteress and a murderer.

Hollywood columnist Sidney Skolsky thought that Phyllis's clingy white sweaters, illuminating her attributes against the gloomy gallows of her Hollywood Hills home, were the irresistible force that led insurance agent Walter Neff (Fred MacMurray) to kill Mr. Dietrichson and allow her to collect on the double-indemnity clause in his policy. The pale blonde wig made her look like a fabulously "cheap dame," but Skolsky could not get over the sweater.

"The sweater," he pondered. "How did the Hays Office ever let that get by?"

"What's wrong with it? The picture is very moral," Stanwyck replied. "It's anti-crime and anti-sweater. It shows what happens if you fall for a gal who wears a sweater."

The sweater was full of dark blood at the end of the movie because the Bad Wife who cheats and kills clearly has to die. Phyllis pleads with Walter. "I've always been rotten," she says, but claims that her love for him has changed her. He can't afford to take a chance on believing her, though. He has paid her a call to kill her, and kill her he does. "Goodbye, baby," he says without emotion, and only a watchful Hays Office edit kept his death in the gas chamber from being equally graphic.

Lana Turner was next to be the blonde bait in white, as Cora in *The Postman Always Rings Twice* (1946), based on another Cain Depression potboiler. Cain had depicted

Cora in Ma Joad-like dresses that gave way to satiny Turner turbans in the cinematic version, but if she was overly fetching for the wife of the miserly old owner of a dusty roadside diner, no matter. The movie was a turning point in her career; in John Garfield's embrace, against the dreary California highway on which Cora died, she showed a reasonable facsimile of acting ability.

As it turned out, the plot of *Postman* was tame compared to Turner's own exploits in and out of marriage. And no one wished her ill in the future more than Barbara Stanwyck. In 1941, Robert Taylor, who happened to be Stanwyck's husband, fell in love with Lana while making *Johnny Eager* with her. She tried to keep things cool; Lana had enough problems with men already. She was

accustomed to the company of her pal Billy Wilkerson, publisher and founder of *The Hollywood Reporter*, and the various tough guys she met through him. Greg Bautzer, a lawyer and sort of "fixer" of legal entanglements about town, had captivated her and then walked out on her. For spite, she ran off to Las Vegas with Artie Shaw on her twentieth birthday and exchanged quickie marriage vows—almost as quick as the divorce proceedings that came through a few months later.

Not long after finding out about her hubby's deep infatuation, Barbara was rushed to Cedars of Lebanon Hospital with severed

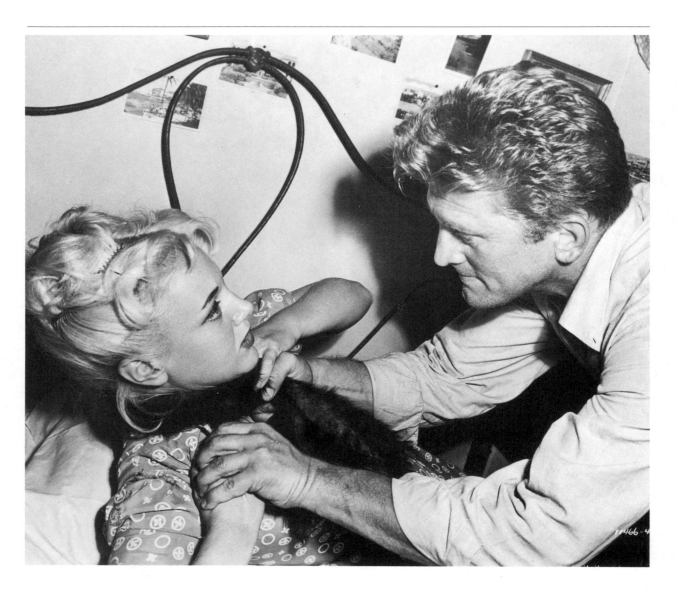

arteries of her wrist and arm. She claimed that she'd tried to open a jammed window, broken the glass, and cut herself. Lana herself tried a similar story 10 years later, after she separated from hubby number three, millionaire Bob Topping. She claimed that she had tried to take a shower while soused, and cut her arm on the glass door.

Twice-divorced Barbara and multi-divorced Lana both spent the Decade of Domestic Bliss, the 1950s, in and out of unpromising romances. Stanwyck went for younger men—including Robert Wagner. The biggest inconvenience to her glitzy

life—her adopted son—was disposed of at boarding school. As a mother, she never was able to "bond" with her child, and when he grew into a fat, homely kid without personality or charm, she may have attempted to give him back to the adoption agency. If she did, the effort failed, so she sent him away and hardly saw him for the next 14 years.

Turner, by contrast, tried to be a good mother to her daughter from her second marriage, Cheryl Crane. Some of mom's friends were an unwholesome influence, however. Her lover, John Stompanato, described at the time as a "swarthy Romeo," had been employed as bodyguard of gambler and gangster Mickey Cohen, and had picked up some useful tactics for getting what he wanted. When he wanted Lana's hand in marriage, and when she refused, he replied that he was sure she'd change her mind—or else he'd cut up her face and kill her. She seemed to be coming around during the eight weeks they spent in Acapulco together, her treat. But on April 4, 1958, a kitchen knife—wielded by 14-year-old Cheryl—put an end to Stompanato's threats, as well as his life. Cheryl claimed during her trial that she was trying to protect her mother. The jury ruled justifiable homicide, but when the judge pronounced the verdict, an unidentified man rose from the gallery and shouted that it was mother-daughter rivalry that had led Cheryl to stab her mother's beau in a fit of jealous rage.

Rita Hayworth, too, had her difficulties as a wife and mother. After her sizzling mock striptease in *Gilda* (1946), in which all she had to do was peel off her satin opera gloves and sing "Put the Blame on Mame" to arouse Glenn Ford's sadistic passions, Hayworth claimed that "every man I ever met fell in love with Gilda and woke up with me."

Charles Vidor, who directed *Gilda*, and Virginia Van Upp, who was the creator and producer, made Gilda's allure a sort of cover for the darker side of the story. With the vicious casino owner Manson (George Macready) safely married to the scarlet-haired seductress, his homoerotic attraction to Glenn Ford became just obtuse enough to escape Hays's comprehension. The happy ending, in which Manson finally does Gilda and Johnny (Ford) the courtesy of dying so that they can live in domestic tranquility, didn't fool anyone but the Hays Office, though. Johnny had already slapped Gilda around and held her prisoner—and since she seemed to respond so well to his discipline, their marriage promised to be full of more of same.

Ford and Hayworth became the era's favorite S & M couple. They reenacted the classic devil-goddess Carmen and her patsy Don Jose in *The Loves of Carmen*, in which,

---

OPPOSITE: *Ace in the Hole*
Jan Sterling is being mistreated by Kirk Douglas. Billy Wilder wanted to show sympathy for her. This is a similar theme where the two lovers try to get rid of the husband for money. Jan said, "To give you some idea of how bad I am, Kirk asked me to go to church with him, I gave him a jaundiced look...I never go to church, kneeling bags my stockings." She wondered what her husband's friends would think after seeing the movie–"He was sure loaded when he married that floozie."

ABOVE RIGHT: *The Divorce Bed*
Barbara Barondess said of her character, "I married for money. I'm on the make for my father-in-law's attorney, Edward Arnold, so that I can get divorced."

capitulating to the more-rigid-than-ever mores of the age, the gypsy and the wasted soldier were married before they took off for the Andalusian hills together. The standard *Carmen* death scene, when Jose becomes crazed with jealousy and stabs her in the bullring, was pure Hayworth-Ford carnal play. He slapped her around again in *Affair in Trinidad*, the *Gilda* rehash that was her comeback after her brief fling at wedded bliss with the Prince Aly Khan. (She was pregnant with her second child during the filming and held her purse over her waistline through many of her scenes.)

Then the baby, Princess Yasmin Kahn, who grew up to look very much like her mother, was born, and the Golden Couple, whose honeymoon safari had appeared on newsreels, divorced. "My husband's far-flung interests and his extensive social interests made it impossible to establish a real home," Hayworth said of her womanizing third mate. She tried again, in 1953, when she married crooner Dick Haymes. He could not hope to ever support the ex-princess in the style to which she had become accustomed, but she kind of liked him, at first, when they met during the filming of *Miss Sadie Thompson*, the third version of the famous Hays Office no-no. While they were in the South Seas, Haymes had some passport problems, and the leading lady took pity on him and got to know him better. As a couple, they "did" Hollywood's nightlife on a regular basis and let Hedda and Louella fawn—until the Westchester County Society for the Prevention of Cruelty to Children found two neglected little girls living in a foster home in White Plains. The chubby, older girl, Rebecca, was built like her famous father, Orson Welles, and her younger half-sister was a princess by birth. Hayworth was

charged with child neglect. Her marriage to Haymes lasted only a few more years. His second wife, Joanne Dru, sued him for default on their divorce settlement shortly after the motherhood scandal, and Hayworth left him broke and in big trouble with the IRS.

The facade of sublime matrimony crumbled even for Hayworth's unruly leading man, who was once appraised thusly by the Duchess of Windsor: "My, you're so homespun!" For years, fan mags had depicted Ford and his wife, Eleanor Powell, and their son sitting contentedly by the hearth in their rustic home. The man who flailed Gilda was said to have turned down a number of movie roles that would have kept him away from his family. But when Powell left him after 16 years of marriage, she said, "He just doesn't care for people."

DUMB BLONDES
AND STARLETS

"I am stupid and I like it. I got everything I want. I got two fur coats....I tell you what I would like. I'd like to learn how to talk good."*

. . . .

The stories had long since become familiar by the late 1940s. Item: Darryl Zanuck, wanting to meet the new contract player, Judy Holliday, who had an IQ of 172, summoned her to his office.

"Stars aren't born. I create them," the mogul pointed out to her.

Then he told her that she was now the property of 20th Century-Fox, and by implication, that meant she belonged to him.

Clash by Night
Keith Andes demonstrates another way to mistreat women. Although Marilyn Monroe only had a small part, she was habitually late, nervous, unprepared, and clumsy. Marilyn herself was nervous at this beginning point in her career as *Playboy*'s famous nude calendar shot was made public. A co-star, Robert Ryan, said, "We tried to tell her off, but we melted. She was so childish, almost angelic and innocent."

---

*Billie Dawn, the dumb blonde, to Paul, the Washington writer, in *Born Yesterday*, 1950.

As he rose from his desk and started toward her, looking hungry, the starlet considered how she had already been made over, chameleon-like, into a Darryl Zanuck product. Formerly a quasi-intellectual Jewish comedienne from Queens, New York, she had been ferried to the back lot laboratories, where she was painted and sculpted beyond recognition with hair dyes, makeup, and prostheses. As the mogul moved in for the kill, she reached down the front of her dress, into her bra.

"I guess these belong to you, too," she said, pulling out her falsies.

Item: Norma Jean Baker, whose natural beauty was as delicately vibrant as the pastel sunrise over the southern California desert, had stripped her hair and tinted her face for Hollywood, and changed her name to the more prosaic Marilyn Monroe. Now she was struggling to keep her rent at the Hollywood Studio Club for Girls out of arrears. She had appeared in *Love Happy*, raising Groucho Marx's eyebrows to new heights of lechery when she undulated into his private detective's office, exclaiming in a mock-frightened, breathy little girl voice, "Some men are following me." For months afterward, she waited for another part, or at least a studio contract, to come along. One day she got a call from a man who said he'd seen her working on the set of *Love Happy* and thought her performance had been impressive. She didn't remember him, but he described a scene in such detail that he *had* obviously been there.

Then he got to the point of the call. He was married, but he and his wife didn't see much of each other. He was lonely. He came to Los Angeles on business frequently, and was wondering if she would be interested in spending time with him when he was there. He would make it worth her while. She could have a Cadillac, or money, or whatever she wanted in return for the favors.

"For a dizzy second I had visions of being able to pay my rent," Marilyn recalled in an interview a few years later. But only for one second. As he went on describing what he would like her to do in return, she squirmed at his frankness. "All I could think of to say was that he shouldn't talk that way over a public telephone."

Instead, Marilyn paid her rent that month by posing for a photographer named Tom Kelley, who was designing a nude calendar. She got $50 for the job and almost ruined her career when the word leaked out two years later.

Item: Vera Jayne Palmer, a lively child with black hair and a precocious figure—at the age of eight, she felt the budding "angel wings" on her chest bounce with her one night when she and the other children in her Texas neighborhood were jumping after fireflies—loved the movies, and was sure that some day she herself would be a movie star. Jayne, as she was always called, almost crushed her ambitions when, at 16, she let a swarthy 24-year-old gas station attendant introduce her to the mysteries of sex. A couple of months later she was sure she was pregnant. She was not about to marry a grease monkey when she was going to be a movie star! Instead, she married Paul Mansfield, a hometown boy with a more promising future. Too late, the "pregnancy" turned out to be merely a scare, but shortly afterward, she got genuinely pregnant by her husband.

When Paul went off to fight in the Korean War, Jayne left her baby daughter with her mother, and took off for Los Angeles. Husband and baby or not, she was going to be a movie star. She got her start by modelling—with and without clothes. Later, Paul and baby Jayne Marie joined her. It was difficult, juggling marriage and motherhood with starletdom, but Paul tried to be tolerant while his wife went out and "worked," packaging herself according to instructions of the publicity agent she hired, Jim Byron. Jayne obligingly bleached her hair blonde, wore decolletages that plunged well below her 40-inch bust, and pulled absolutely any publicity stunt that dreamed up by Byron. One of his early brainstorms was to get her into the offices of several local newspapers during the Christmas holidays, where she would slip up behind a few tired city room male reporters, hug and kiss them and give them some "Christmas cheer." The stunt got her photograph seen all over the country. In 1954 Jayne and Paul split up, and with only a brief pause for regrets, she went on doing *anything* to become a star.

Holliday had been a brief but shining light on stage. Monroe tried time and again—by studying serious drama, by marrying the era's most lofty American playwright—to show that she had substance behind her sex appeal.

The Big Knife
Shelley Winters portrays a frustrated starlet in this film with Jack Palance. Winters commented: "I was originally brought out west by Harry Cohn. They made my hair pink and tried to make us all look like Rita Hayworth."

Mansfield was exactly what she appeared to be, except with a shrewd adding machine of a brain. But in the Hollywood of the 1950s, a bosomy blonde—whether bosom and blondeness were natural or not—was destined for a one-note career. She could be the eternal starlet—the big, busty, sexy little girl who was a Sex Toy to all men. If she didn't want to do that, she could go back to her hometown and hope some potential husband or boss would take her seriously. Even that could be difficult, as Joan Marchesani, a newly hired ticket agent with Pan American World Airways in New York City found out the hard way in 1958. As *The New York Times* reported: "Miss Marchesani had served 87 days of her 90 day trial period...when a supervisor objected to her platinum dyed hair, her professional type of makeup and her figure hugging sheath dresses. The 20-year-old girl, who resembles the actress Kim Novak, wiped off all her makeup except her lipstick and agreed to wear the airline's blue grey uniform. But she drew the line at changing her hair color to strawberry blonde." So the supervisor dismissed her on the grounds that she was "too pretty," although the union interceded on her behalf and she was eventually reinstated.

In Hollywood, a shapely "girl" had a chance—a chance to be judged by a higher authority than an airline supervisor. Darryl Zanuck's assessment of his employee Marilyn Monroe was "just another easy lay." Harry Cohn fondled the photos and the flesh of any number of young hopefuls in his search for a new and hopefully more compliant version of Rita Hayworth. "He tried to groom anyone who came along to be another Rita Hayworth," Shelley Winters said.

Harry the Great bought *Born Yesterday* for Hayworth and Bogart, but his red-haired siren ran off and married Aly Khan and "retired" before the shooting started. When Garson Kanin suggested Judy Holliday, who had lucked into the role of the dumb-blonde-with-a-past on Broadway and proved that Jean Harlow's brassy, sassy spirit lived on in spite of a decade-and-a-half of humorless goddesses, Cohn reportedly replied, "Don't waste my money. You don't seem to understand. On the stage you can get away with a broad who looks like that, because the audience sits far enough away, but with the camera movin' in, she'd drive people out." For lack of a better choice, he finally

capitulated and hired her after all. Holliday won the Best Actress Oscar.

Lorelei Lee, the first dumb blonde, may have been a creation of the 1920s, but on the way to the age of Sputnik and suburbia, her hormonal wiring underwent some alterations. Part of the inspiration for the Sex Toys of the 1950s came from Marie Wilson, who starred in unmemorable movies in the 1930s and 1940s, playing a vacuous blonde in low-cut gowns, then became a big name in the late 1940s, when she starred in a CBS radio series called *My Friend Irma*, which later moved to television. As Irma, she was a secretary too daft to chew gum and polish her nails at the same time. "No stunt was too crazy, no cheesecake too cheesy," an interviewer once said of her. *Time* magazine ran this piece of fluffery on her in 1947: "She has been playing

OPPOSITE: *Gentlemen Prefer Blondes*
Both versions show gentlemen in compromising situations. It began as a comic novel with the title *The Hasty Traveller*. It was serialized in *Harper's* and translated into fourteen languages. Author Loos met with Dr. Lin, a Chinese scholar, and asked him how a country with no blondes could understand the concept. He relied, "Blondeness is not resigned to pigmentation." Ruth Taylor (in the 1928 version) followed the philosophy in the movie: she married a millionaire and lived happily ever after. Alice White (also in the 1928 version) gave an interview in the 1970s to two young men and at the conclusion she said: "I've done you a favor. Why don't you do one for me and let me give you a blow job?" They declined. Darryl Zanuck had originally cast Betty Grable in the 1953 version but then decided to use Marilyn Monroe due mostly to financial considerations: Betty Grable would have to receive $150,000 and Marilyn Monroe could be paid only $18,000. (She did demand and get her own dressing room.) Jane Russell was paid $100,000 to play her bosom buddy. Zanuck didn't really believe that Marilyn was singing her own songs and made her perform for him privately. The film works because the female friendship is number one in the film. It's also true that Jane befriended Marilyn and escorted her to the set. After co-star Tommy Noonan said that Marilyn "kissed like a vacuum cleaner," Jane comforted her. Director Howard Hawks admitted that the film might never have been made if Russell hadn't befriended Monroe.

Phffft
Does Jack Carson have bad breath? Not one of Judy Holliday's most captivating roles because Harry Cohn decided to make her into a sexpot by dressing her in strapless dresses and turning her hair platinum. She said, "I'm happy to play a writer wanting to be passion's plaything." Writer George Axelrod said, "I'm trying to smash the myth that laughter and sex don't go together....I'm striking a blow at the double standard because the wife does the playing around." In preparation the studio wanted some sexy shots so cameramen told Ms. Holliday to wet her lips and open them, but she looked only vacant. But one day the photographers were discussing a meal and Judy got the lustful look they required. Thereafter, whenever they needed a sexy shot of her, they showed her a menu.

the role of a dumb blonde for so long that she now lives the part. Marie's fluffs at rehearsals and on the air are daffier than anything a scripter might imagine. 'She is so much like Irma,' says Sy (Howard, the show's writer, director and producer), 'that I have to rewrite the things she says to make them believable.'" In fact, other accounts of her said that people who knew her described her as "smart, witty, and kindhearted."

Then Monroe came along and reincarnated Lorelei Lee, complete with Wilson-style cheesecake shots, in *Gentlemen Prefer Blondes* of 1953. Lorelei was still a gold-digging showgirl, easily brought to heights of ecstasy by the sight of a diamond tiara, but now there was a difference. Whereas gold-digging screen sirens in the Jazz Age and the Depression would scoff at the thought of true love, the man behind the Dun & Bradstreet rating could turn the new Lorelei to mush as quickly as his wallet could. She meant it when she told the disappproving father of her pallid, bespectacled fiancé, played by Tommy Noonan: "Don't you know that a man being rich is like a girl being pretty? You might not marry a girl just because she's pretty, but my goodness, doesn't it help?"

On the heels of Lorelei and her diamonds, Marilyn married another unsizzling nearsighted chap, played by David Wayne, in *How to Marry a Millionaire*, and here the truth was out. The Sex Toy was available to any male—he didn't have to be rich *or* handsome, and he could even be a bit of a bruiser, as Robert Mitchum showed in Marilyn's next movie, *River of No Return*. Marilyn told a reporter that she was thrilled to finally have a "real man" in Mitchum, but then it was back to being Everyman's plaything. It was a lucky decade for Tom Ewell, who should have played nothing but kindly uncle roles, but

instead was tempted by Marilyn in *The Seven Year Itch*, and married Mansfield in *The Girl Can't Help It*, a lowbrow version of *Born Yesterday*. In *Bus Stop*, Marilyn succumbed to the lasso of a gangly, gauche cowpoke played by Don Murray, who held her captive until she decided he was a nice guy after all, able to love her in spite of her career as a tuneless chanteuse/B-girl. (In later years, when the world learned that the ex-Miss America and New York City commissioner Bess Myerson had tried to lasso a lover back into her clutches, albeit with phone calls and letters instead of a rope, the press and public would pronounce her behavior obsessive and unsound.) It was the leading lady who was supposed to overtake the screen; her leading man's sex appeal was moot. His job was just to be male.

In 1953 Harry Cohn was smarting. It was all over a photo—of the new Lorelei Lee, effervescently smiling with Marilyn's luscious lips. Marilyn had sent him the photo with the inscription, "To my great benefactor, Harry Cohn." It opened up an old wound for Cohn: four years earlier, when the great MM was still a struggling starlet, he had been unimpressed with her screen test at Columbia. He wasn't sure she was pretty enough, and besides, he had said, "She can't act." Six months after that, Marilyn was a star, and the property of 20th Century. Now, Zanuck laughed in Cohn's face when Cohn asked to borrow her. Harry called his casting director, Max Arnow, into his office and commanded: "Get me another blonde!"

Arnow produced Miss Deepfreeze of 1953, a recent arrival from Chicago named Marilyn Novak, who took her first screen test in a strapless gown designed for Rita Hayworth to wear in *Gilda*. Harry was unimpressed at first, but he finally decided to make her over.

"Bring me your aunt or your sister, and I will do the same for them," he told reporters after he had made his latest ingenue a star.

Of course the name had to go; the town wasn't big enough for two Marilyns. She fought to keep her last name, and won, but everything else was designed by Cohn. She played blondes of easy virtue in *Phffft* (the title refers to the sound of a marriage going flat), *Pushover*, *The Man with the Golden Arm*, and *Of Human Bondage*, but in private, Cohn did his best to keep her romances cool. He didn't want her to get married, because that was how he had lost Rita, his goldmine. Kim felt like a freak when Uncle Harry had the studio hairdresser tint her hair lavender, to set her apart from the blonde pack. Swathed in chemical solutions that day, Kim learned an important lesson: for a blonde in Hollywood in the 1950s, there was no such thing as too unnatural. Mansfield seemed to understand that dictum instinctively. Once she had perfected a platinum shade for her own hair, she went to work on her menagerie. Jayne rarely traveled without an entourage of flunkies, lovers, children, and pets, and when she went to New York to audition for a Broadway show, one of her companions was a pink poodle on a leash. This was designed for maximum tasteless effect, since she had flown east only at her agent's insistence. Jayne's aim was to be a movie star—what good was a mere Broadway play to her? So she did her best to horrify the New York artsy sophisticates, dressing in pure Hollywood trash-chic, pink poodle and all. As luck would have it, however, the producers of *Will Success Spoil Rock Hunter?* were looking for a Hollywood sex bomb to play the role of Rita Marlowe, the Hollywood sex bomb. The role, on stage and later on the silver screen, practically made Jayne's career. And little

female baby boomers across America added pink stuffed poodles to their toy collections.

If the blondeness was designed to make the Sex Toy as synthetically luminous as the afterglow on Bikini Atoll, the breasts made her a Venus for the Atomic Age, a vision of woman evolved to mutant proportions for the pleasure of grownup baby boys. "Men must have thought breasts were like pyramids, pointed and everything. There was this special brassiere at Universal that made you pointed," Mamie Van Doren recalled years later. In the forgettable *High School Confidential*, in which she played the blonde nymphomaniac aunt and guardian of a boy who turns out to be a narc, she wore a clingy turtleneck that made her breasts point out like missiles ready for blast-off. Cleavage was still riskily risqué, so side shots of her "pyramids" under wraps were substituted.

Into this breast-obsessed culture, *Playboy* was born in December 1953. Feminist writer Barbara Ehrenreich theorizes that the fantasy life Hugh Hefner fashioned on the magazine's pages—ultra-trendy playboy pad with a picture-window view of brightly lit urban skyline, a new curvaceous playmate every night—was an answer to the mature man's discontent. By the 1950s psychiatry had developed a massive weight of theory establishing that marriage—and with it, the breadwinner role—was the only normal state for the adult male. Men who rejected the mature family provider role were considered afraid of the responsibilities involved. The flip side of adult responsibility, from the male perspective, was the male rebellion that launched the "right" to shed the yoke of obligation by frolicking with well-stacked nubile young Sex Toys—or at least with four-color centerfolds if commitment barred the possibility of an actual toy of one's own. The

The Naked Kiss
Constance Towers had her head shaved by her pimp as
punishment for organizing his girls to walk out on him. She
beats him savagely with a telephone and takes his money. The
director, Samuel Fuller, states Kelly's feelings: "What a thrill it
is: when you get through laying any of these bastards he pays
you off and leaves. You don't have to listen to him or his stories
or his lies." Ms. Towers spoke of the effect on society: "I want
to play good girls in movies. I think a great deal of juvenile
delinqency stems from glamourization of the bad girl.

Playmate's come-hither expression told every
man who took a peek that she was his for the
duration of his fantasy. You couldn't bring a
Sex Toy into your real life after all. She would
never fit in at family Christmas dinners or
PTA meetings.

One of *Playboy*'s favorite toys through the
1950s was Jayne Mansfield. The first time she
posed for Hef's photographer, in 1955, she
wore pajamas that she raised over her tits.
Then she became a mainstay of the February
issues, appearing in 1956, 1957, 1958, and
again in 1960. While Marilyn had worried
that posing as a plaything would destroy her
career, for Mansfield it became a vehicle to
carry her to stardom. Kim Novak also found
that posing for *Playboy* didn't hurt her public
image.

Monroe, on the other hand, gave the Sex
Toy new dimensions in the public mind by
exposing her desire to be taken
seriously—baring it, however inadvertently,
far too much for her own good. The
vulnerability of the sex symbol who wants to
be more became Marilyn's appeal, and if her
vulnerable quality has made her a cultural
icon to this day, it also has made her the one
immortal, eternal Sex Toy, with a body and
mind ever available for public scrutiny.

Early on, Marilyn's vulnerability seemed
exploitable. In 1951, Zanuck agreed to try her
in her first challenging role, in a movie in
which she was to play a babysitter trying to
protect her charge from a madman, to be
played by Richard Widmark, who was
running loose in a large New York hotel. Yet,
by the time the movie, *Don't Bother to Knock*,
was released the next year, Marilyn had
become the disturbed young girl who teaches
Widmark, the hero, a lesson in pathos.

Marilyn obligingly gave interviewers such
quotes as, "If you're a blonde it is considered
that you have to be told what to do, that
someone else has to decide things for you."
The world grew to understand that the
glamourous MM's image as sex queen was a

facade for an insecure, lonely little orphan girl desperate to be loved and appreciated—and eventually, the woman behind the facade became a part of the facade. Fans first began to understand the complexities of Marilyn as a Sex Toy when her dream marriage to Joe DiMaggio collapsed after only a few months. "Friends report they were bored with each other...He called her a nag..." the newspapers reported. *Bored* with Marilyn Monroe? Of course—who had ever said there was a solid, substantial woman beneath the bewitching shell? The word was out: Marilyn needed a man who could help her develop her potential to love and to think, and protect her from the Hollywood sex-symbol-machine. Men all over the world fantasized about taking on the job.

It became clear that the goddess-as-victim-of-Hollywood's-inhumanity was even sexier than the almost-bare Sex Toy as a flat and silent full-page glossy in *Playboy*. For three decades, Will Hays had tried, as head flack man for Hollywood, to promote a positive image through the press and the movies, but his efforts all went down the tubes in the 1950s. It was a difficult time for the studios, with competition from the *enfant terrible* known as television, with the fanatical eye of Senator Joe McCarthy on every writer, director, actor, and crew member who had ever dabbled in progressive political ideas. Because the studio heads were not courageous about standing up to the House Un-American Activities Committee, they created the liberal-sacking blacklist to police themselves against prosecution, just as they'd created the Hays Office to protect themselves from censorship. But because people went to movies for insights that television did not yet offer, and because stories about greed and

corruption in Hollywood only seemed to make the public more curious about the tormented psyches of their favorite stars, it seemed perfectly okay to serve up Sex Toy starlets as vocal opponents of the Hollywood machine. Marilyn could tell the press whatever she wanted about the way Fox

The Girl Can't Help It
Jayne Mansfield is shown here with gangster boyfriend Edmond O'Brien, who told an agent, "all you've got to concentrate on is to turn this dame into a big canary in six weeks." When Jayne attended the preview she confided to her escort that since she and Marilyn Monroe were both under contract to Fox she was another Monroe. Even Hugh Hefner got in a jam over nude photos of Jayne, and he was booked on two counts of obscenity. In 1962 her husband hit her when her dress fell to the waist, but in 1959 she had refused to go nude at a beach, stating: "Too bad I'm not Marilyn Monroe. She's a naturalist. I'm sorry."

victimized her; all Zanuck asked was that she show up for work. (More and more frequently, she didn't.) On the screen itself, Shelley Winters as Dixie the starlet in *The Big Knife*, explained her real job: "They hire girls like me to entertain the visiting exhibitors. They louse you up, then they call you a louse."

And Zanuck went right on ordering girls to be delivered to his office like pizza. Jerry Lewis made *Ladies Man*, it is said, just to supply himself with starlets. Kirk Douglas once jumped a costumer who had entered his trailer to assemble his wardrobe, assuming any woman in his territory was there for the business of pleasure. Even at the height of stardom in the late 1950s, Marilyn is reported to have been requested to "entertain" studio execs.

Of course, a Sex Toy with box office clout could always rebel. Fox repeatedly suspended Marilyn for failure to report for duty, repeatedly took her back, and every little tiff between studio and star made headlines. Kim Novak's first trip to Europe gave Harry Cohn a few sleepless nights. She was supposed to be showing off to the press at the Cannes Film Festival, but there, before Uncle Harry's eyes, in black-and-white, was a headline proclaiming "Kim and Aly Are On a Spree." Not another star hooked up with Aly Khan! He phoned Muriel Roberts, the studio publicist who was supposed to be Kim's duenna and protector on this jaunt and screamed at her across the a continent and an ocean. "There is nothing to it," insisted Muriel. At last she managed to calm Harry down, but the next scandal may have been enough to wreck the mogul's health. During the Christmas holidays of 1957, Dorothy Kilgallen heard a rumor—a tidbit the backbiting columnist simply couldn't resist,

about Kim Novak and *Sammy Davis, Jr.* This at a time when a black-white coupling was still called miscegenation. Whether they were, as they claimed, "just friends" or had, as the mushrooming rumor claimed, actually taken out a marriage license, Kim was whisked into seclusion for a couple of weeks, Sammy unexpectedly married a black chorus girl and separated from her seven weeks later, and Harry Cohn had a heart attack when he heard the first rumblings of the news at a holiday gala. On the flight back to L.A., where he intended to mobilize a "mob" of connections to stop this romance, he collapsed again, but nevertheless went right to work when the plane landed. In February 1958, Cohn received a package of clippings about the Kim-Sammy story. He sulked for three days before he had another sudden heart attack—this one fatal.

Harry Cohn dead? Kim, who heard the news on the set of *Vertigo*, was aghast. "This is the end of a way of life," said many at Columbia. The last of of the Harry-made sex bombs felt a pang of guilt, wondering if her recent brouhaha had been enough to stop his heart. Then she let Alfred Hitchcock and Edith Head transform her once again—to a sophisticated blonde with elegant makeup and couturier fashions. For Kim, this was indeed the end of a way of life.

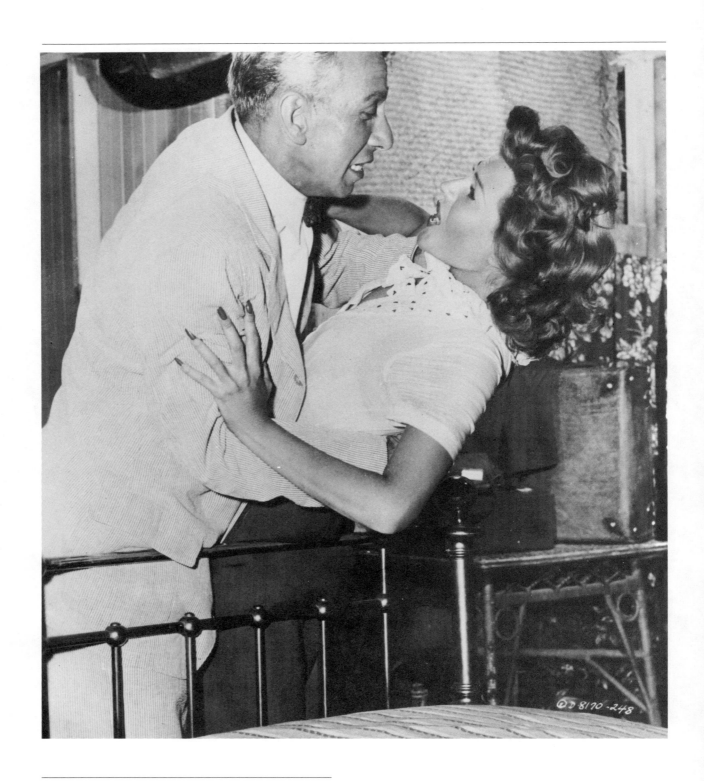

Miss Sadie Thompson
Somerset Maugham said that Rita Hayworth was his favorite
Sadie. Harry Cohn disagreed with Rita about her look in the
film, saying: "Her past should only be shown in her clothes,
not her face."

BAWDY BORDELLOS, PARTY GIRLS AND THE REVOLUTION

"You're still the same. You're nothing but a prostitute!"

. . . .

Otto Preminger was determined to make a cinematic adaptation of *The Moon Is Blue*, a popular Broadway comedy by F. Hugh Herbert. The story of an innocent young damsel and a philandering man of the world who end up falling in love had some "shocking" dialogue—the good girl made such startling pronouncements as "I'm a virgin" and "You're trying to seduce me!" So naturally, the Motion Picture Producers Association (MPPA), as it was now called, waited to see a revised, whitewashed script. This was a common practice.

Except that this time, there was no revised script. Preminger refused to change a word of the original, bellowing something about "artistic integrity."

With those marching words on his breath all the while, he went ahead and produced the

movie. William Holden, cast as the leading man, was a major box-office draw, so Preminger had an idea that Holden's popularity would prove irresistible to exhibitors whether he got a Production Code seal or not.

Preminger won his gamble. Maverick exhibitors did show the film, released in 1953, and audiences trooped past picket lines of Legion of Decency supporters to see it. The picketers had taken their annual pledge in the Catholic Church, in which they vowed: "I promise to promote by word and deed what is morally and artistically good motion picture entertainment. I promise to discourage indecent, immoral, and unwholesome motion pictures....I promise not to cooperate by my patronage with theaters which regularly show objectionable films." Thus, it seemed their duty to discourage this one.

What the audiences saw was an utterly innocuous moral parable of rake meets good-girl, fails to bed her, and so marries her—yet they were watching motion-picture history in the making. Here was one more major puncture in the iron rule of the Production Code Administration. If Otto Preminger

---

Jose Ferrer, as reformer Alfred Davidson, to Rita Hayworth, as Sadie, in *Miss Sadie Thompson*, 1953.

though still playing a lay reformer rather than a reverend, finally, after three decades of silence, spelled out Miss Thompson's occupation. The Breen Office had been growing increasingly impotent as movie audiences saw rape discreetly flaunted in *A Streetcar Named Desire* (1951), a Tennessee Williams-eye view of sexless marriage, *plus* a hint of fellatio in *Baby Doll* (1956), and drug addiction graphically depicted in Preminger's seal-less *The Man With the Golden Arm* in 1956. When Fred Zinnemann directed *From Here to Eternity* (1953), the PCA was disturbed less about the New Congress Club, described as "two steps up from the pavement," than about watching Deborah Kerr and Burt Lancaster commit adultery on the beach while wearing bathing suits. Zinnemann refused to throw robes around them, as the PCA requested, but the movie got the seal anyway. When David O. Selznick was making the 1958 version of *A Farewell to Arms*, and wanted to have his wife, Jennifer Jones, walk into a red velvet room with a large ornate bed and mirrors on the ceiling, and remark, "I feel like a whore," Geoffrey Shurlock, who was director of the Production Code Administration then, sympathized. Shurlock ended up deciding that if the word "whore" was good enough for the Bible it was good enough for him. He was horrified at the public outcry.

didn't need the PCA seal, if Howard Hughes had finally distributed *The Outlaw* in 1947 *sans* seal, and made a killing at the box office after six years of bickering with Hays, Breen and company over the camera's mesmerization by Jane Russell's breasts, who *did* need the Production Code?

The risk of federal censorship died for all practical purposes in 1952, when the Supreme Court tried the case of Roberto Rossellini's *The Miracle*, about a simple-minded peasant woman who fancies that she has been seduced by St. Joseph and had a child through divine conception. New York State censors had banned the film as "sacrilegious," but the court, in a unanimous opinion, declared that movies were entitled to guarantees of free speech. So much for the power of state censors if the Supreme Court was not prepared to uphold their decrees.

As a result, the same year that Maggie McNamara said "seduce," Rita Hayworth starred in the third film version of the notorious *Sadie Thompson* and Jose Ferrer,

Once again, to cut or not to cut had become one of the hottest issues of the decade, and the next one, as debate dragged on well past 1968, when Jack Valenti, the new MPPA head, chucked the whole seal of approval business and began the X, R, GP, and G rating system for movies. Enlightened parents began to wonder if PCA-endorsed movies had led nearly a whole generation of girls to believe that kissing a boy could make you pregnant, since three minutes of kissing was all it took in the movies. Judith Crist took a celebrity poll in the August 1969 issue of *Good Housekeeping* magazine, in which the former taxi dancer Billie Cassin, now of course, the *grand dame* Joan Crawford, said, "I think sex is the most beautiful, wonderful, exciting thing in the world, tender and lovely and very personal, but it should be done in the home and not projected on the screen in such vulgarity."

By then, the whole Hollywood structure had metamorphosed from the days when

BELOW: *From Here to Eternity*
Donna Reed works at the New Congress Club as a hostess entertaining Montgomery Clift and Frank Sinatra. Discussing the role of Alma, for which she won an Academy Award, she said: "I don't approve of her or her way of life but I discovered that she can give valuable tips to almost any woman."

OPPOSITE: *Revolt of Mamie Stover*
Why did Mamie Stover have to leave San Francisco? In this bordello scene, Agnes Moorehead explains some of the rules to her "girls." Discussing her career, Jane Russell explained that "I fight against being sold as a sex personality, but I don't care if I represent good or evil...as long as the story has the proper moral." Jane Russell is now a minister in the Pan American Church.

young hopefuls like Billie could be signed to a studio and become its creation. A 1948 Supreme Court decision was a landmark victory for an antitrust suit against Paramount. The Court declared block booking, the fixing of admission prices, unfair runs and clearances, discriminatory pricing, and purchasing arrangements favoring affiliated theater circuits to be illegal restraints of trade. The Big Five studios (Loews, which owned MGM; Paramount; RKO; 20th Century-Fox; and Warner) were ordered to divest themselves of all pooling arrangements with movie theaters. Over the next decade, district courts ordered further prohibitions against the studios that made the movies also controlling distribution in theaters. As a result, the exhibitors gained the right to show whatever movies they wanted—and that included low-budget "art films" in which nudity and graphic language were considered as sacred to the *auteur*'s self-expression as to Michelangelo's *David*, and racy depictions of existentialism from those ever-in-the-vanguard Europeans. No code tampered with sexual realism in these films, and the Hollywood blockbuster, faced with stiff competition, was forced to grow up.

Preminger, known henceforth from *The Moon Is Blue* as a man who took risks, chanced a plunge in his personal life, into the bed of a statuesque black leading lady when he brought back the world's favorite bitch-goddess, Carmen. This time it was an all-black folk opera titled *Carmen Jones*, which had been a resounding success on Broadway a decade before. Carmen was transported to mid-America during World War II, working in a parachute factory and seducing not Don Jose but plain old Joe, a military policeman, leaving him for a boxer instead of a toreador. Preminger didn't think the elegant Dorothy

Dandridge, who had made a name for herself as a singer, was right for the part at first. He wanted a hussy.

But Dorothy was hoping against all the odds to get this role. She had one unpromising interview with Preminger, but he agreed to audition her. "I hurried to Max Factor's studios and looked around for the right garb. I would return looking like Carmen herself," Dandridge said in her autobiography. She went to the gym and worked herself to exhaustion before she went to see Preminger again. "As a final bit of staging I arrived a little late," she recalled. "I arrived at his offices, passed by his secretary, and dashed inside. 'Oh Mr. Preminger, please forgive me....I just got back....I am not dressed....'"

He looked at her and said, "My God, it's Carmen!"

When she did get the role, Dandridge worried that she might offend the black community because it showed a black woman as willing strumpet. Preminger talked her back into playing Carmen over steaks and champagne at her house. He also told her that an intimate relationship with the producer could help an actress bloom before the camera.

As she vamped Joe, played by that 1950s' heartthrob whose appeal crossed all color lines, Harry Belafonte, Dandridge had visions of finally overcoming all the barriers that had slowed her career progress—and of thumbing her nose at all the high-placed white men, among them Harry Cohn, who had relished the idea of a black mistress or one-nighter, but not a wife. The Academy of Motion Picture Arts and Sciences wrote her name down for posterity as the first "Negro" ever nominated for an Oscar for acting in a major role. She didn't win, but the nomination

seemed like enough at the time. By then, she had her mind on her three-year contract with 20th Century, and on Otto. He had made the down payment on her handsome new home in the Hollywood Hills, and somehow, she thought that this time things would be

Carmen Jones
Ruby Dandridge, Dorothy's mom, told her, "I know how you can get that part," and she showed her how to do "switching" (which was the method of moving her behind sideways) like the street women, and told her to "use a petulant attitude."

ABOVE: *The Balcony*
Workers in what was called the screen's first "surrealistic bordello" were played by women of twenty-one different races and nationalities in this film based on the play by Jean Genet. Shelley Winters played the madam, and said: "I like playing a madam. Everything in the script has two meanings — fantasy and reality."

OPPOSITE: *A House Is Not a Home*
Over three million copies of Polly Adler's autobiography were printed after members of the Algonquian Roundtable urged her to publish it even though it was her thesis for UCLA. The actresses agreed to appear in it because good movie roles were hard to find, people didn't confuse them with the roles they played, and the pay was great. Shelley Winters, who played Polly, said: "I wanted to give her...dignity....I sat next to her at the premiere of *The Balcony* — she was incensed at it. I personally don't think she had any sex life at all. She got into the business by hanging around dance halls."

different—that he would leave his wife and make their affair legal.

Dandridge, who had studied at the Actors Laboratory with Marilyn Monroe as a classmate, saw her career and her personal life peak and fall with *Carmen Jones*. On Otto's advice, she turned down the next role that 20th Century offered her, and soon found herself without him and with no more picture offers. Later she went bankrupt thanks to some bad investments, lost her Hollywood palace, and turned to pills. She ended up thinking of herself as not so different from the classic kept black woman of the Old South. "I learned that the same thing applied to me as to any good-looking washwoman or houseworker in Mississippi: you can be used but don't expect to be received publicly and legally as a wife," she said before she died of a drug overdose in 1965, at the age of 42.

The tragedy of the platinum Sex Toy that Monroe and Mansfield became in real life, and the dusky version that Dandridge tried so desperately not to be, was that they were too closely associated with a 1950s' vision of women to ever escape it, even when the next decade brought a new crop of screen goddesses who behaved more or less like a man's equal in the boudoir. A celluloid whore of the 1950s, on the other hand, seemed perpetually destined for an unhappy ending. *The Revolt of Mamie Stover* (1956), starred Jane Russell as a buxom redhead who played "hostess" to 51,840 GIs at The Bungalow dance hall in Honolulu's Iwilei district. Mamie makes a killing with the help of a world war, and uses her earnings to buy up enough of Honolulu to qualify for membership in the most respectable country club—but the tweedy novelist she loves won't marry her because of her occupation. The hula dance contests that exhibitors staged as

an "exploitation extra" to go with the cinematic attraction, however, went a long way toward popularizing all things Hawaiian on the mainland, so that by the time the island paradise became a state in 1959, the whole country was enraptured with grass skirts, the ukelele, the hula, and of course, the hula hoop, for anyone of any age whose hips needed remedial training.

Meanwhile, the "party girl" returned to the screen. Here was an updated flapper, post-Kinsey Report. She was libidinous and given to drinking all night, just like her 1920s' counterpart, but whatever her parents' socioeconomic status might be, it didn't matter because she depended on her own resources for support. She was as likely to have a job as not, depending on her mood, and she might try exchanging sexual favors for money, as much for the sake of adventure as for survival. Carolyn Jones was a party girl circa 1957 in *Bachelor Party*, Paddy Chayevsky's tale of five men trying to cope with the heady responsibilities of breadwinnership, seeking temporary escape in booze, stag films, and beatnik girls. Jones, as an emissary from the carefree planet of Greenwich Village, wears a clingy black turtleneck sheath and sleeps with her 60-year-old landlord to keep from having to pay rent. She's living a life of delusions, as it turns out. She thinks all men are crazy about her—but in the world she inhabits, men are free to have women without putting on shows of romance and passion. Men are free to show that they find her tedious—just as men find all women a tedious responsibility in this screenplay.

The time seemed ripe for a prostitute with a streak of independence. She arrived with the new decade, in the form of a lanky beauty with exotic, craggy features, a sporting and unrepentant import from Greece named Illia, played by Melina Mercouri in *Never on Sunday*. Illia, a legend in her own time around the Piraeus waterfront, was known as a whore who "makes no prices, she has to like you."

Jules Dassin, a blacklisted American director, made the movie in Greece with $150,000, starred in it because he couldn't afford to pay a leading man, and ended up grossing about $6 million, as well as marrying the internationally desired Mercouri. *And*, the Screen Directors Guild honored Dassin as a "brother" once again shortly after the movie was released. The blacklist was beginning to crumble to, at least for those exiled Hollywoodites who had managed to keep from disintegrating when they found themselves suddenly and inexplicably without work or friends in Lotus Land. The *Never on*

Sunday story of the darling of the docks and the amateur philosopher from Connecticut named Homer, who wants to salvage the purity that was once Greece by reforming Illia, has overtones of *Sadie Thompson*, but with a more wholesome aura to the relationship. Homer is enchanted to find that Illia speaks several languages—she learned them in bed—and that her favorite way of relaxing is to watch the Greek tragedies—until he finds out that she has twisted every tale in her mind to give it a happy ending. He embarks on a mission to change her life-style through education, rather than the word of God, and keeps a tight rein on his desire to sleep with her. Though Illia gives serious consideration to reforming, she finds a more pressing outlet for her particular moral nature—the "girls" who are more or less the white slaves of Mr. No Face, the gangster landlord who charges them exorbitant rents, need a leader. Only Illia dares stand up to No Face, so she agrees to go back to the whoring life to act as union negotiator for the other women. In the end, Tonio, the Greek-Italian laborer who loves her, carries her off, away from Homer, with a hint that love will stop her from the life after all. Yet the word "marriage" is not explicitly stated.

Americans were enchanted, and preserved the memory of Illia by buying the rousing *Never on Sunday* soundtrack. Hollywood sensed the start of a trend. The scripts could say such words as "whore" and "sex." The

Party Girl
In this gangster story set in Chicago of the 1930s, Cyd Charisse dances twice. She said, "I never thought of taking the movies seriously. Director Nick Ray made *Party Girl* at the same time he was barred from the set of *Wind Across the Everglades* for being drunk.

157

fashions of the new decade—clinging chemises; hair teased and tousled in imitation of that sex kitten from France, Brigitte Bardot; thick black lines around the eyes—made women look wanton anyway. The time was ripe, and if ever there was a golden age of hooker movies, it was the early 1960s.

At first, the traditional endings, and the theme of P with an H of G and a longing for respectability seemed important. "I virgin," Nancy Kwan tells William Holden when they met on a Hong Kong ferry in *The World of Suzie Wong*. Of course, he soon finds out that she is a yumyum girl in the notorious Wanchai world of bordellos and dance halls. Holden heroically stands up to the Crown Colony's racist society and marries Suzie, but even with reform through the love of a good man, she has to receive an extra whammy of punishment and watch a ferocious landslide devour her baby boy—as though an ethnic stepson is a bit too much for the controversial element of mixed marriage. Kwan, who is half Scottish and had learned to speak the King's English in a convent school, worked at perfecting a Cantonese accent for the role. The colorful *cheongsans* that Suzie Wong wore—silk sheaths with mandarin collars and skirt slits eight inches up from the knee—became a hot fashion item among American women, but the garment industry here sewed up the slits so that they reached only a modest two or three inches above the knee.

Elizabeth Taylor died remorseful in *Butterfield 8*, and won a PCA seal for the

Bachelor Party
Carolyn Jones said that the "just tell me you love me, you don't have to mean it" line was the reason she was nominated for an Academy Award.

160

movie as well as an Oscar for herself. But neither she nor Geoff Shurlock wanted any part of the movie at first. When the head censor saw the first version of the script, based on John O'Hara's 1935 novel based on the diaries of a murdered flapper, he reported in a memo: "We have the feeling that the characters in this story are preoccupied almost exclusively with sex....appear to talk about nothing but formication...are shown indulging in sex on numerous occasions." After months of negotiations, scriptwriters Charles Schnee and John Michael Hayes reduced the party girl Gloria's nymphomania to simple promiscuity, and got MPPA approval. But the problems only began there. Producer Pandro Berman had bought the story with Taylor in mind, and she was stuck with doing one more movie for MGM, at a paltry $125,000 salary, before the studio would end her contract and release her to make *Cleopatra*, for which 20th Century had offered her $1 million. In Taylor's eyes, it was all too evident that MGM wanted her to play the lusty Gloria to capitalize on her own indecent exposure in gossip columns around the world, when Eddie Fisher, best friend and protegé of sorts of Liz's late husband Michael Todd, had left Debbie Reynolds for her.

He Who Must Die
Melina Mercouri tells the following story. After *Never on Sunday*, a journalist ogled and pinched her and tried to make a date. "At first I was outraged, then I say to him, 'okay, geev me your telephone number and I call you...oh nooo not your work number, your home number,' and he gets scared and nervous, and shaky." Roaring with laughter, she also said: "I do not want to work here [in the United States] because the studios offer me the same part — the harlot with a heart of gold."

"The script is pornographic," Liz declared. "The leading lady is almost a prostitute."

Sol Siegel, the head of MGM production, retaliated with a threat to suspend Liz and legally prevent her, under the terms of her contract, from working for another studio for two years.

"If you think I've been trouble in the past, you just wait," said Liz. As consolation, Berman agreed to let Eddie play the role of Steve, Gloria's platonic musician friend, even though he considered Fisher a drug addict *and* a lousy actor. Liz and Eddie both received speed-laced injections from filmdom's Dr. Feelgood, a physician named Max Jacobson, during the filming, and Liz developed half-a-dozen illnesses, but Gloria became one of films' most beloved harlots.

In *Elmer Gantry*, Burt Lancaster played a lecherous revivalist preacher who was able to live out any fantasy Alfred Davidson, Sadie Thompson's would-be savior, ever dreamed of having. "He rammed the fear of God into me," noted Shirley Jones, playing the bordello dweller who had met him when she was an innocent.

Around this time, Dr. Harold Greenwald

ABOVE LEFT: *The Key*
Sophia Loren is available to any man who receives the key to her apartment. She was concerned about William Holden's coldness during filming, as he confessed, "beautiful women throw me." On the set, one of the crew showed a bare-breasted photo of Loren. Holden was upset until Loren proudly declared, "They look pretty good to me," and that broke the ice.

LEFT: *Zorba the Greek*
Lila Kedrova, shown here telling Anthony Quinn about her past life, won an Academy Award for her portrayal of a dying prostitute. Kedrova commented: "This woman was sleeping deep in my heart and she just had to wake up and begin to move. Everyone liked *Zorba*, but when I saw myself on the screen I wanted to become a nun, I was so ugly."

had written a best-selling psychoanalytical study of "what makes women become prostitutes," entitled *The Call Girl*. It became the 1960 movie *Girl of the Night*, which told the melodramatic tale of a high-priced call girl named Bobbie, played by Anne Francis,

The World of Suzie Wong
Here's a confrontation between the good woman and the bad girl. Nancy Kwan wanted to wear a slip in a scene but was forced to wear bra and panties. She said, "I can't wear these clothes," but producer Ray Stark said, "Look, you're not Nancy Kwan, you're Suzie Wong." She replied; "I hope they won't believe this in Hong Kong."

who looked like a Vassarite, lived in a posh building on New York's Upper East Side—and had a pimpish boyfriend who sponged off her substantial earnings. She wound up neither reformed, killed, nor punished, but instead, sorting it all out on an analyst's couch, talking about the father and mother who abandoned her, and trying to grasp the idea that men might like her for herself rather than just for her body. A small burst of excitement broke out in Youngstown, Ohio, when an exhibitor used a business card with Bobbie's name on it as a promo tool, and a local vice squad thought the cards belonged to a real hooker, but in general, the movie did poorly at the box office because audiences found the docudrama approach too depressing.

Grim or not, the bad-girl-on-the-analyst's-couch would return. Once the country's inhibitions crumbled enough to accept the idea that money might not be her only motivation for entering the profession, the working girl's psyche—particularly those deep, mysterious recesses that had caused her to enter the life—turned out to be just as titillating as her body. "A man may fall in love with a prostitute and want to figure out the 'what's a nice girl like you doing here?' syndrome, especially if he's met one who's good at the job," explains Dr. Samuel Janus, a psychotherapist who has worked extensively with prostitutes in New York City. "If she's smart, she plays innocent, maybe even telling the man she's there only because of some tragedy in her life or a dire need for money. She does that because it makes her client feel that he's someone special to her—a strong protector."

Billy Wilder, a director who liked to spit in the eye of restraining conventions, created a benign group of Parisian *mecs* (pimps) in *Irma la Douce*, which starred Shirley MacLaine as a streetwalker who wants the naive *gendarme*-turned-pimp, Jack Lemmon, to prove his love by roughing her up once in a while. Before they marry and go straight, Lemmon and the *mecs* find themselves in need of shelter from the law, so they form a protective association called the Mecs Paris Protective Association, which by sheer coincidence, happened to have the same initials—MPPA—as a certain overprotective association in Hollywood.

A year later, Wilder released an even more farcical—and less funny—picture called *Kiss*

Me, Stupid, at the most inopportune possible time—the week after Legion of Decency pledge day in the Catholic Church. It wasn't so much the belly-button rhinestone worn by Kim Novak, as Polly the Pistol, that the legion wished to obliterate as the plot line, in which seedy songwriter Orville J. Spooner's (Ray Walston) neurotic jealousy leads directly to his *wife* (Felicia Farr) turning a trick with none other than Dean Martin, playing himself, when a detour brings Dino to their hometown of Climax, Nevada. Poor half-baked Spooner is torn between his possessiveness and his desire to seize the moment and attempt to sell Dino some of his

OPPOSITE: *Elmer Gantry*
The camera as voyeur lets us look in through the window as Lulu's plans for revenge through blackmail come together by having a photographer snap her and Elmer Gantry together. After the movie was released, Shirley Jones said: "I haven't been home since....but I got letters from mothers of teenaged daughters, saying 'you were my daughter's idol, how could you degrade yourself?'"

ABOVE: *Rear Window*
A voyeur enjoys a peek at a party girl.

more notable songs, such as "I'm a Poached Egg." He's even willing to serve up his wife to the womanizing songster if it will help his lackluster career, as long as she isn't his *real* wife. That's where Polly the Pistol comes in. Her flesh is for sale, so Orville hires her to pose as his wife, and cooks up a fight with his real missus, Zelda, so that she'll go home to her mother for the night. Orville reaps his own undoing, however. He finds himself getting jealous of Dino's interest in his fake wife, throws his celebrity guest out of the house, and right into Polly's room at the local Belly Button Cafe, where Zelda happens to have also found herself detoured. The next morning Zelda is $500 richer and unremorseful. But Wilder remade the sequence in between Martin's entrance at the cafe and Zelda's exit to ward off a "Condemned" rating. Originally, there's a strong hint that Zelda and Dino are awake much of the night together, but in the expurgated version, he clearly falls stone cold asleep.

Truman Capote created a sophisticated party girl with few scruples about promiscuity in his novella *Breakfast at Tiffany's*. When he thought of Holly Golightly he thought blonde, with soft, vulnerable edges. The equation pointed directly to La Monroe, and Capote had talked to her about playing the role. But higher authorities at Paramount had a different idea of what the 1961 party girl should look like. Holly became the sleek gamine Audrey Hepburn, an actress with a far more self-assured aura than Marilyn. Holly didn't even need a stalwart and solvent man to do her thinking for her, as the Sex Toys did. In the dubiously fairy-tale happy ending, she runs off with gigolo/writer George Peppard, a man no better prepared to take on the cruel world than she is. But the new party girl

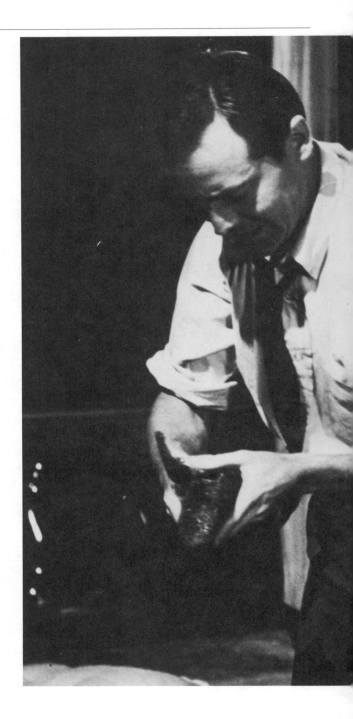

Girl of the Night
The girls prepare for the worst in this semidocumentary of call girls in the big city. Anne Francis comments that the film "sounds like one of those movies on lower Times Square....It's the most challenging role I've ever had....Dr.Greenwald told me some places to go — but if I stayed up 'til two in the morning looking at them, I wouldn't do so well playing one the next day."

169

could always get by, somehow. Hepburn, whose feathery frame was an opposing force to Marilyn's voluptuousness, made the American woman want to be tough inside and delicate outside. Hepburn grew up to be ultra-slender because she was a victim of starvation in her native Holland during World War II; when she became the new American ideal, women here started limiting their daily caloric intake to war ration levels.

In real life, pre-mod London had two party

girls whose lives were not unlike Holly Golightly's for a few wild, ebullient years. Christine Keeler and Mandy Rice-Davies tried a little promiscuity with powerful men, a little prostitution, a few orgies here and there, a smattering of drugs and black lovers, and a Svengali touch from a well-connected osteopath named Stephen Ward. In 1963, however, after a falling-out with Ward, Keeler told all to the yellow press, including the story of her simultaneous affairs with a suspected Soviet spy and the War Minister, John Profumo. The scandal brought down the Conservative government, after 13 years in power. Dr. Ward was convicted of "living off immoral earnings," but committed suicide before he was sentenced. And London's image around the world began an abrupt about-face, from staid to swinging. London had rock'n'roll. And party girls and boys. And ultimately, it had the Siren for the Sexual Revolution—Julie Christie.

Darling, for which Christie won the 1965

Oscar for best actress, told the story of Diana Scott, a vacuous party girl who drifted through life modeling, acting, tormenting the man she loved, and bedding with cold but influential Laurence Harvey, who holds a mesmerizing power over her and her show-biz career. Christie saw the character as a composite of Christine Keeler and a few other lustful but empty London "birds"—but while Keeler has ended up dejected and broke in a British government-owned council flat, Diana ended up dejected and married to an Italian prince. Christie's genteel face with the sensuously petulant lips turned up in photo spreads all over the world, modeling the new London look of micro-skirts, shimmery lip-gloss and yards of long, flowing hair. She also talked, mostly about life as a free-spirited, modern woman who was much more interested in securing a foothold within the artsy set than in being a movie star.

She quickly made it clear that Julie Christie, not Diana Scott, embodied the new London chic. "I think [Diana] was just the

---

OPPOSITE, TOP: *For Pete's Sake*
In this film it's all very whimsical, nothing is very overt. Barbra Streisand has been busted after she goes into hock to the mafia and goes to a cat house. Director Peter Yates liked that Barbra asked so many questions about the film. His purpose in making films? "To entertain — no message intended."

OPPOSITE, BOTTOM: *Irma la Douce*
Shirley MacLaine discusses her career: "The only good parts I ever got were hookers. Naturally I took them because I wanted to be successful. That's why I'm an expert in hookers. That's why I'm an expert in doormats. That's why I'm an expert in victims. They were the best parts. And when I woke up — socially, politically, and creatively — I could no longer take those parts and look in the mirror."

ABOVE, RIGHT: *Kiss Me, Stupid*
In an unusual scene, Felicia Farr as the "good" wife meets Kim Novak, the "bad" woman. After the wrap party, Novak commented: "I don't know if I'll ever work again."

Among the guests at this party are Martin Balsam as a movie producer who has a yen for Holly Golightly (Audrey Hepburn), Holly herself, and her boyfriend, kept man George Peppard. Hepburn was persuaded to to take the part by director Blake Edwards. Hepburn stated: "Many girls have lived like her, and I myself lived in circumstances very much like Holly. I didn't have to look far to understand the character....I was luckier...I earned a bit on the side posing for pictures, advertising soap." She told reporters that "Holly was really a frightened mouse who never delivered, even if she grabbed the $50 bills." Truman Capote, who wrote the novella, said, "I mistakenly sold the movie rights to Paramount. They made a big boring Audrey Hepburn thing out of it."

least swinging person I know," Christie said. "Her friends were all squares...they were just depraved more than anything else. I think it's rather old-fashioned to be depraved." Christie later became active in various political causes, but in the mid-1960s, a swinging mod sex symbol was rarely asked about her views, except on the issue that seemed to be the most explosive domestic issue in the Western world—sex.

Christie's politics were that she lived with her boyfriend, Don Bessart, an art teacher who worked as a mail carrier part-time. They had met when he had brought her a letter. She told the press that marriage could ruin a great love affair. "I refuse to compress myself into conventional mediocrity," she said. "Men don't relish responsibility, and neither do I."

The media also dissected the sex life of Jane Fonda, who by the mid-1960s was starting to emerge as America's homegrown sex symbol for revolutionary times. The world knew that she had an IQ of 132, had attended Vassar, and measured 36-21-35. She had played a giddy young brothel employee in *Walk on the Wild Side*, had received the *Harvard Lampoon*'s award for worst actress of 1963, and gone on to a number of semiclothed roles that could have branded her as a mindless sex bomb, except that, even while she was leading the *dolce vita* in Paris as Mrs. Roger Vadim, she tended to be willing to speak out on sex as an issue—from the radical point of view.

She had lived with Vadim before they married. In the changing times, *Cue* writer Jesse Zunser wanted to know how Fonda felt about "the argument that a man who gets free samples when he wants them feels he doesn't have to buy the merchandise, and the man who sees that a girl's a pushover for him may feel she'd be a pushover for others, too—before and after marriage."

"A man will marry a girl if he loves her," Fonda replied, and sent the youth of 1964 pondering. "The sex incident has nothing to do with it. Sex is a part of love, but love is a lot more than sex."

The Production Code collapsed around the same time that America's youth began to see all of the establishment's ways as flawed. Sex wasn't immoral; escalating troops in Vietnam was. Settling down to the straight-and-narrow path of marriage and making

TOP: *Darling*
Julie Christie, who won an Academy Award for her performance, commented: "Whatever I am, I am not Diana. I suppose what I really dislike about Diana is that she doesn't use her noggin. *Darling* is a satire on a very real world but a world I'm thankful I don't know at all, the Christine Keeler world!"

BOTTOM: *Scandal*
Mandy Rice-Davies (Brigitte Fonda) is served; the notion was that the man in the mask was royalty. Twenty-five years after the scandal, the movie was made. The producers spent six years developing the script, as they had planned to put it on British TV, but censors wouldn't allow the story of a "Commons call girl" on the telly. (Does this mean that the Pamela Bordes story will be a movie soon?)

money didn't lead to fulfillment. The same adults who railed against the *avant garde* drugs of choice were likely to stew their brains with a three-martini-lunch habit. The motivation behind the movement was not the same as the post-World War I sexual emancipation that led to the flapper cult, but as far as the movies were concerned, all roads seemed to lead to heady hedonism.

There were happenings instead of speakeasies, acid trips instead of hallucinogenic gin, bikers in search of meaning instead of bootleggers in search of profit. There were moral endings in the movies, still, but what was morality? Nowadays, nice girls from respectable families *did*. People wondered if commercial sex would disappear now that it was becoming widely available as a free staple.

Instead of disappearing, however, the working girl became, for perhaps the first time since the days when demimondes of the ilk of Camille and Nana were fixtures of nineteenth-century Left Bank life, an accepted, if not fully welcome, addition to the counter culture. As movies showed it, anyone who could thumb her nose at the establishment's values, and make a living on the fringe, must have something to contribute to the new order.

Shirley MacLaine came back from meditating in India, where she was thrown in jail during a Himalayan mystic revolution ("I don't understand exactly what that is myself,"

Walk on the Wild Side
Capucine portrays a very unusual working girl, as she's a sculptress and intellectual, but she must be punished in the end. According to co-star Anne Baxter, Laurence Harvey said Capucine couldn't act and stormed off the set. Capucine cried for a week.

LEFT: *Midnight Cowboy*
There's a misunderstanding between Sylvia Miles and Jon Voight. Sylvia Miles stated: "I can't imagine why anybody would try to hustle me, since I got nominated for a six-minute hustle."

BELOW: *Breakfast at Tiffany's*
Patricia Neal writes a check for George Peppard's services.

she told reporters) to star in *Sweet Charity*. A Bob Fosse musical version of Fellini's *Nights of Cabiria*, *Charity* is actually a simple dance-hall-hostess-meets-man-who-can't-bring-himself-to-marry-her-after-all tale except for the exuberant song-and-dance, and the distinctively 1969 ending. After falling asleep for the night in Central Park, Charity Hope Valentine renews her hopes for happiness not through the saving grace of a lover or reformer, but through a little love, spread by a roving group of flower children who stop and regale her with posies and love beads. She can always give up the Fan Dango Ballroom and join a commune. The bordello itself went psychedelic in *Easy Rider*, and Jon Voight, as a hustling party *boy* in *Midnight Cowboy*, found himself getting stoned with the Beautiful People.

In the movie marketplace, the "art film" had been an important cultural iconoclasm in the sexual revolution, depicting sex, and using once-forbidden language with frankness and consistency. But the 1960s were a time when anything that became popular outside the establishment was quickly picked up by some clever packager who would remodel it for the mainstream. It happened to pot paraphernalia, which was gussied up for the head shop, and to faded blue denim, which began to show up on every fashionable posterior complete with designer logo and price tag. And it happened to the art film, which went mainstream by keeping the shock value and easing out the artiness. Exploitation films come in many guises today, but some of the earliest mass-distributed art-evolving-into-soft-core-porn brought back those wild and crazy party "chicks" from Europe—Camille and Carmen. Director Radley Metzger used performers who, as is typical in porn, only a masochist can enjoy

Camille 2000
Danielle Gaubert doesn't even cough in this version. Asked about nudity, she said, "Oh, I'm really quite shy, but I suppose I would do a nude scene if it was a good director and the scene belonged in the film."

watching as they attempt to act, but gave amusing modern twists to *Carmen Baby* and *Camille 2000*. "This *Carmen* is closer to the novel than any other movie version," said Metzger. How so? He brought back the jailbird husband that Prosper Mérimée gave Carmen. The 1967 Carmen doesn't have to bribe officials to get hubby out; she just participates in a *menage à trois* with the judge and his wife. She leaves her Jose for a rock singer instead of a bullfighter. Camille of 1969, on the other hand, has become a junkie instead of a consumptive.

By 1973, when *Deep Throat* became the first hardcore porn movie to enter

177

ABOVE: *Pretty Baby*
In this child auction scene, Brooke Shields has just been sold as
a virgin. Shields was impatient with those who worried about
her playing a child prostitute, and asking the same question —
"Do you think you will become Violet?" Director Louis Malle
said that "Frenchmen never had a penchant for young girls. It's
an English, American, and Italian inclination."

RIGHT: *Foxes*
The teenaged girls identify the body of their friend, who was
hooking and hooked on drugs. Foster said of her role: "I hate
to sound egotistical, but it's the best performance I've given,"
but "I never went through any of that. I never went to a rebel
high school, never wore...funny hairdos or rode in vans, so it
was different for me."

mainstream distribution (followed years later by Linda Lovelace's revelations that her director/husband, Chuck Traynor, had forced her, through constant beatings and threats of more, to star in porn movies and be a virtual white slave to his lascivious whims, including a sexual encounter with an animal), prostitution had become a sometimes uneasy part of the feminist agenda. Aligned feminists, and feminist prostitutes, who were themselves organizing groups such as COYOTE (an acronym for Call Off Your Old Tired Ethics), which called for an overhaul of public views and for national decriminalization of prostitution, noted that it was the male establishment that had divided women into madonnas and whores.

For the most part, the women's movement agreed that as long as men were society's powerbrokers, there would be a customer base for prostitutes, because a "trick" pays a prostitute for the favor of giving him complete control. "Some women would rather be prostitutes than spend their whole lives debased in a marriage. There's the myth, of course, that prostitutes are badly treated by pimps, but I'll bet as many men abuse their wives as pimps abuse prostitutes," says feminist lecturer and activist Florencey Kennedy, who has worked with prostitutes' rights groups since the early 1970s.

Yet at the same time, Margo St. James, who

Taxi Driver
Jodie Foster said, "I spent four hours with a shrink to prove I was normal enough to play a hooker. I didn't see myself as a baby hooker but as a runaway." She did research by getting into satin hot pants and walking for a month on New York City's Lower East Side. Her mom, Brandy Foster, said: "I couldn't believe how she looked in that wardrobe, suddenly she had legs. I was happy when she returned to her grubby little self."

179

180

founded COYOTE in 1973, has said that prostitutes, like men, view sex as power, which makes them seem a threat to both men and women. The working girl's power lies in the fact that she presumably doesn't have to live her life by a man's rule, and she can command compensation for the sexual hold that women have over men.

Throughout the 1970s, the Hollywood screen was moving away from the harlot-as-damsel-in-distress image. By virtue of youth and some special circumstances, a couple of preadolescent actresses played roles that presented controversial exceptions. When

OPPOSITE, TOP: *The Happy Hooker*
Lynn Redgrave explains why she accepted the role: "It's why I became an actress. I wanted to play people and characters far removed from myself, and let's face it, I can't think of anyone further removed from myself than Xaviera Hollander." During filming, Lynn got a request to do a promotional shot to publicize voter registration and since Xaviera herself was not allowed into the United States or Canada, Redgrave wryly asked: "They couldn't deport me for playing Xaviera, could they?"

OPPOSITE, BOTTOM: *Hustle*
As in *Klute*, both call girls marry the cops who protected them. Catherine Deneuve comments on her character: "I know girls like this. I understand them...how they feel when they reach a state that the only commodity they have to sell is themselves. One is kept by a man and then discarded and then the process begins again. There's a market for that."

RIGHT, TOP: *Steelyard Blues*
Jane Fonda's blackeye is courtesy of a trick. Another actor in the film, Garry Goodrow, said that this was to be seen as *cinema verité*. Fonda's feminist consciousness began when working on the film and she to noticed the ways men treat women condescendingly.

RIGHT, BOTTOM: *Klute*
Jane Fonda fought with director Alan J. Pakula because she wanted a less traditional ending. Roger Vadim said earlier that when Jane saw women sitting in the windows in Amsterdam she exclaimed: "It's shameful to degrade women like this! A whore is a human being, not a creature that you exhibit like an animal at a fair."

Brooke Shields starred in *Pretty Baby*, the story of a child who grows up in old Storyville and knows no other life, rumors flew that Brooke's mother had sold her 12-year-old daughter to the celebrity flesh peddlers. A *Newsweek* writer asked Brooke, who was not yet allowed to date but had posed for *Penthouse*, about her views on the profession of the character she played. "Prostitution is bad, but it was a little different back then," she said. "There was a family feeling and only certain gentlemen were allowed to come in. Now you just stand out there and anyone can come and you can get killed."

In *Pretty Baby*, the child harlot ends up trying, along with her mother, to adapt to life in a proper home. Iris, the runaway street slave that Jodie Foster, then 13, played in *Taxi Driver*, also went back to her parents and her school, but the horror of a girl so young hustling in Times Square, with a pimp forcing her to go out and ply her body, was hard to forget. One who didn't forget it was a psychopath named John Hinckley, who became obsessed with Foster, terrorized her with incoherent fan mail, and brought the movie back into the news when he shot President Reagan in 1981, ostensibly, in his clouded mind, to become a hero and impress Foster the same way that Travis Bickle the

OPPOSITE: *McCabe and Mrs. Miller*
Julie Christie portrays an opium-addicted madam who rationalizes to Shelley Duvall: "Look at it this way: you had sex with your husband in exchange for your bed and board. Now you're a harlot and you take money. Small difference."

RIGHT: *Back Roads*
Sally Field discusses her character: "Amy is also kind of flakey. Amy's different. I can't even begin to describe how different she is. She's a totally other human being who I have never met before."

taxi driver had become something of a celebrity when he shot Iris's pimp. People wondered if playing the role of a streetwalker had made Foster easy prey for a madman.

On the other hand, Xaviera Hollander claimed that harlotry could be a terrific life for a consenting adult in her book *The Happy Hooker*, which quickly became a movie starring Lynn Redgrave. The celluloid Xaviera goes into the trade after a dashing lover convinces her that she should not find it degrading to accept a cash gift that is simply a token of his appreciation for a romantic week together.

Cinderella Liberty
Marsha Mason, an Academy Award nominee for her role, said: "I liked her. I found myself defending her....I mean, they call her a terrible character, a whore, a prostitute, a terrible mother. She wasn't. I'm sick and tired of seeing women being empty-headed. They fail, lose, or die. I'm not asking for hearts and flowers, but if you see a character go through a tremendous amount of pain you should let her grow." The film's title? Navy slang for a pass that expires at midnight.

Jane Fonda observed that making a living off such favors was a difficult life, for which one had to develop a tough hide, when she prepared for her role in *Klute* by spending a few weeks around the women who cruised the after-hours bars. "I made Bree much more vulnerable than a real prostitute would be. A real character would have been difficult to make sympathetic," she said later. The script had Bree explaining to her psychiatrist that her profession had an addictive aspect; she enjoyed the adventure and the control over clients. But *Steelyard Blues*, the less successful movie that Fonda made with Donald Sutherland and a group of friends from her FTA show in 1972, on the heels of her Oscar for Klute, had a more political whore. FTA, a troupe composed of counterculture actors, stood for either Free the Army or Fuck the Army, depending on one's preferred perspective.

Fonda herself was developing her feminist awareness at the time, and she demanded that a bar scene with a topless dancer be purged from the *Steelyard Blues* script. (From the movie, she went on to become an active COYOTE supporter.) Her politics were, of course, notorious by then, and when the band of thieves, a hooker and other assorted rogues escaped the police blockade at the end, the group of real cops who had been assembled for the scene shot at her with fake bullets and whooped it up, shouting "Kill that bitch!" and "Get her!" and such. But that was only a private fantasy of a few fanatics; the audience had seen the lawbreakers win in the end. The celluloid hero no longer had to be an upstanding citizen, and the heroine no longer had to hanker after a life of virtue.

Best Little Whorehouse in Texas
Dolly Parton felt that playing a madam was bad for her image until Burt Reynolds persuaded her. Later she commented, "Miss Mona is a lot like me. I get a chance to dress up the way I like with crazy wigs and the wild clothes and everything juiced up [a gesture toward her bosom]. I like the freedom of speech in the movie, being able to talk the way I talk, I can say hell or damn if I want to!"

186

UNDRESSED
FOR SUCCESS

She had some lean times when she started up, but she wanted a prestige business, and she knew it depended on the "look" of the girls. Soon she was running three agencies—Cachet, Elan, and Finesse. Much of her interviewing was done in a basement office on 79th Street between Madison and Fifth. One young woman—call her Pamela—remembers phoning Finesse a year ago and being asked to go for a "looksee," a fashion-biz phrase for a model's audition. She was asked to provide two pieces of I.D. and to "come dressed as if your grandfather was taking you to lunch at '21'."

Half a dozen girls were there when she arrived. Several who were unsuitable were politely asked to leave. Much to Pamela's chagrin ("I am rather proud of my dress sense—my father was a diplomat"), she found herself being inspected by Sheila Devin for shaved legs, then being criticized for the height of her heels (too high) and the hue of her pantyhose (too flagrant).*

. . . .

More than a century before blueblood Sydney Biddle Barrows left her $12,000-a-year job as an accessory buyer in New York's garment district to become a fast-track entrepreneur, under the nom de brothel Sheila Devin, the cattle barons of LaGrange, Texas (75 miles down the road from Houston), were reveling at the local legal pleasure palace—actually a rustic ranch house with the lustiest trollops in prairie country. Scarlet lanterns had burned there since 1844. During the Depression the madam had allowed struggling farmers to pay for the girls' services with chickens; hence it became known as the Chicken Ranch.

The last madam at the Chicken Ranch was a rawboned, grandmotherly Texan named Edna Milton who had started as a "girl" at the age of 16 and risen through the ranks. "My reasons for going to La Grange were all financial," she told a magazine interviewer. "My three month old marriage had broken

*From "The Story of the 'Mayflower Madam'," by Anthony Haden-Guest, *New York* magazine; December 10, 1984.

up. I only got married to get out of the house anyway. I was on my own with a limited education and had to work to go to school, only I couldn't get a job 'cause I wasn't 18. Ya can't do both."

Edna Milton's guests could lounge about the parlor on bar stools that rested on two well-proportioned female-shaped legs. The madam paid her taxes and contributed to the

RIGHT: *I'm No Angel*
Mae West said, "I'd never play a madam. That's even more despicable than a pimp. A prostitute, well, maybe she's oversexed or something."

ABOVE: *Glad Rags to Riches*
Shirley Temple was taking dancing lessons at The Children's Dancing School when an agent spotted her: "I'll take the one hiding under the piano!" These parodies of the latest film stars made a couple of years before she went to kindergarten, border on kiddie porn. Temple said they "were one of the best things I ever did." The code forced her to clean up her image.

local Little League. Everyone had a rollicking good time until the early 1970s, when a grandstanding television reporter named Marvin Zindler "discovered" that Texas had a legal whorehouse. He claimed that it was a multimillion dollar arm of the Mafia.

Zindler's "scoop" led him to hound Governor Dolph Briscoe into action. On hand to cover the sudden epidemic of morality that closed the Chicken Ranch in 1973 was Larry L. King, who sold the tale of the legendary Chicken Ranch to *Playboy*. From the pages of *Playboy* the Ranch found its way to the Broadway stage, in *The Best Little Whorehouse in Texas*, a play that celebrated harlotry and reviled hypocrisy through a foot-stomping country-and-western score by Carol Hall. From there, Universal Studios started talking screenplay with Burt Reynolds and Dolly Parton, and dealt a round of punches to the show's creators. King made a few snide cracks about Burt's receding hairline and Dolly's wigs, and Burt sent him a missive challenging him to a fistfight. But in 1982, after many mishaps, the Ranch came to the silver screen.

As work environments go, there was never a grander place to punch a timeclock than Dolly Parton's place. In the dark ages of 1955, a dancing scene outside a brothel in *Oklahoma!* had been abandoned on the cutting room floor, but now, the prairie peaches came out from their rooms and danced down the staircase. (There had been no second story, and no staircase in the real house, but this was Lone Star Victorian-style bawdy house frills as only Hollywood can do them.) Did the bowlegged buckaroos come for sex, or to see a chorus of beautiful girls who seemed destined more for Broadway than the boudoir? As long as the Chicken Ranch was accepting applications, no

TOP: *Risky Business*
Tom Cruise becomes an entrepreneur by opening a bordello in an affluent suburb. During casting, director Paul Brickner interviewed two hundred actresses: "I wanted the hard edge of sexuality for that character — someone who was not really warm and not really accessible. Rebecca De Mornay said her character "was equally a part of me as the high-class hooker."

BOTTOM: *Eating Raoul*
According to co-star Mary Woronov, who said her character was "cunningly naive," the film was inspired by the TV sitcom, *The Honeymooners*. In this scene, she and co-star Paul Bartel have just killed Garry Goodrow by hitting him over the head with a frying pan.

sagebrush belle in her right mind would settle for the lot of the good woman in town. The local hash-slinger, played by Lois Nettleton, was dried up and burnt out, with carnal yearnings that had passed her by. Sheriff Ed Earl (Reynolds) preferred Dolly. Only for the madam would Mr. Macho put on black bikini underpants.

Dolly herself thought that the role might not be good for her image when she first received the offer, but Burt talked her into it. She liked her sequined, clingy, tarty wardrobe. "The hookers are still the flashiest gals this side of Hollywood," she told a reporter.

Parton's flashy trash was fine for cattle country, but it wouldn't get an upwardly mobile 1980s' whore into the circles in which proper urban clients mingle. If there's a moral left on the screen today it is this: if you want to wake up in a penthouse, don't dress like a cheap dame. The celluloid hooker today doesn't have to thumb her nose at society's standards; in the face of Contragate and Wall Street's insider trading scandals she looks, to many observers, like the last bastion of integrity. She has a responsibility now—to show all the ex-counterculturites who like to think that bowing to the corporate world constitutes "prostituting" their finer instincts that whoring isn't necessarily a dirty word, but rather a job filled with intrigue and high-powered clients. In short, she's something of a role model. It's reassuring if a role model looks stable, dependable, prosperous, and prepared for a long, productive career. How can you look reassuring in a flimsy, skintight sequined dress and skyscraper pumps that teeter under your curves? A more sobering reflection of the times is that to be successful as a man's fantasy sex object, it helps to look clean—as clean and AIDS-free as any girl

who lived next door and went to work for IBM.

In *The Verdict*, 1982, Charlotte Rampling was barely recognizable as a whore. She looked elegant and earnest in her pinstripe suits, toting her briefcase, baring an intellect honed by law school. But why should she dress in garb that will set her apart from others in the legal profession? After all, in her world, everyone is a whore, except Paul Newman as a down-and-out lawyer about to regain his self-respect by suing the negligent medical staff that left his client a vegetable. If her own father (James Mason) is a whore for the system, happy to defend the criminally negligent for the right price, why should a sexy lady lawyer have any scruples about using her wiles to seduce Newman and report his plan of attack to the defense team? What a choice assignment—go to bed with Paul Newman and be paid well for it.

"You look well tended," William Hurt, as Ned, a seedy Florida lawyer, tells Kathleen Turner, as Matty, a woman who has chosen to be a rich wife instead of a lawyer or stockbroker in *Body Heat*, 1981. Director/writer Lawrence Kasdan was imitating the old James Cain film noir pulp style, but in the 1980s, men know better than to fall for dames in tawdry sweaters. On a sweltering night, Matty is wearing white designer chic. Apparently, she's shrewder than the tarty Phyllis of *Double Indemnity* in every way; Matty ends up happily alive on some exotic island, while her lover takes the rap for her husband's murder.

Kasdan, more famous for *The Big Chill*, is one of Hollywood's new generation of filmmakers who are known for sleeping with scripts instead of starlets, and for making movies that reflect the disillusionment of today's bourgeois adults who believed, 20 years ago, that when they grew up they would save the world. When *Body Heat* was released, Kasdan told an interviewer that the character of Ned was inspired by Kasdan's observations of frustrated ex-'60s' college students. The mediocrity of adulthood, he said, had led many to "this casting about for quick solutions to their own happiness. Suddenly they're looking for that great business deal or that great scam that is going to make them a mint and buy their freedom." The yuppie hooker of the 1980s has found the perfect scam in the world's oldest profession, the eternal option. And as a proper upper-middle class teenager in *Risky Business*, 1983, Tom Cruise tries pimping and gets into Princeton because of his precocious business acumen. He's able to report to the Future Enterprisers Club, a group of kids eager to learn the fine art of capitalism, "My name is Joel Goodsen. I deal in human fulfillment. I grossed $8,000 in one night."

Paul Bartel and Mary Woronov, a couple who began their careers in the underground film circuit of the 1960s, invented a repressed but ambitious couple who are a send-up of everything greedy about the 1980s in *Eating Raoul*. Paul and Mary Bland don't like sex, but then who ever said that swingers-for-rent have to like the work? All they want to do is get rich enough to buy a restaurant. Their scam is enticing obnoxious debauchers with cash-filled pockets and "gourmet" sexual tastes to Mary's lair, where she waits in basic black leather, then killing the client and grabbing the cash before Mary actually has to submit to the horrors of flesh upon flesh. They even get away with it. "If we'd been killed or punished at the end, it would make the crimes real," says Woronov. "But we made the movie like a cartoon. I mean, killing someone by hitting him on the head with a

Indiana Jones and the Last Crusade
Alison Doody explains her motivations to her victims, as she has been intimate with father and son, rationalizing, "I'd do anything for the Holy Grail." Speaking about the character she plays, Ms. Doody said she liked the way this woman "manipulated men and situations."

frying pan—that only happens in cartoons."

Other prominent yuppie hookers of the screen have found that their greatest occupational hazard is a murderer out to punish them. A partial roster: Kathleen Turner in *Crimes of Passion*, 1984, stalked by the crazed preacher Anthony Perkins. Sigourney Weaver in *Half Moon Street*, 1985, the whore with a Ph.D to replace a heart of gold, with a spy ring out to kill her. Donna Wilkes, in *Angel*, 1983, as the abandoned baby fast-tracker hustling on Sunset Boulevard to pay her tuition at North Oaks Prep School, terrorized by the assassin disguised as a Hare Krishna, only very loosely based on the real Hollywood strangler. Sean Young in *No Way Out*, 1987, a Washington mistress with a biting wit that could have landed her a job writing for *thirtysomething*, slayed by her sugar daddy, Gene Hackman. Barbra Streisand in *Nuts*, 1987, a Jewish American Princess netting $100,000 a year from "friends"—and only if she likes them—who finds her sanity on trial when she kills a trick in self-defense. As though a hooking career isn't action-packed enough even without the chase scene! After all, for these pros, it isn't just a business, it is theatre.

As the career woman with a dual identity in *Crimes of Passion*, for instance, Turner puts on a show in the red light district every night. Director Ken Russell saw hooking as her freedom of sexual self-expression. By day, she was Joanna the sportswear designer, dressed in androgynous greys and button-downs—an ensemble that would brand any real-life fashion designer as uncreative. By night, she donned a wig, went down to her crib, and gave a man whatever he desired. Originally, her services included handcuffing a cop to her bed and probing him with his nightstick, all at his request, but Russell cut that footage to

secure an R rating instead of an X. Such a variety of scenarios—and for payment, as proof of her talents—are, of course, not something a fashion designer often has the opportunity to star in, but how was China Blue able to express her own lusts by acting out her client's fantasies? They were still the executive producers and she the leading lady.

By 1980, when Brian De Palma tarted up his then-wife Nancy Allen ("I really don't know why two sensitive, intelligent people get divorced," he mourned to a *Wall Street Journal* reporter later in the decade) for *Dressed to Kill*, the Hillside strangler had held Los Angeles streetwalkers in terror, and other mass murders of prostitutes in other parts of the country, not to mention what seemed like an increase in random acts of rape and murder of women, had made frequent headlines. Angie Dickinson played the cheating wife whose white designer dress is hacked to bloody pieces in an elevator, and Allen, as a call girl whose real passion is buying real estate, is next on the killer's list.

OPPOSITE, TOP: *Half Moon Street*
Sigourney Weaver said, "I read the script and it was controversial at the time. I thought it was great. There have been so many movies about a double life — normal women in the daytime and whore at night....What I admire about Lauren is that she leads her life. She doesn't try to keep things separate. She uses her own name and goes to work in ordinary clothes. She becomes quite infamous and very successful as an escort even though she's fairly intimidating....She really is independent. She doesn't want to lead a normal life and she won't....I've met part of her in women but I've never met the whole package.

OPPOSITE, BOTTOM: *Crimes of Passion*
Kathleen Turner said, "Some people told me not to do it, but my husband said he saw the challenge. I'm more an actress than a sex star. I don't feel akin to China Blue. That woman was so afraid. She was anxious to find someone to tell her she had power. I did *Crimes* because I had a chance to act my ass off."

By then a number of feminist activists around the country were denouncing the pornography industry for glamourizing violent sexual dominance against women, and possibly rousing some male viewers to action. De Palma's films, which rate an R for their sensual nudity, graphic and often surrealistic violence, but with sex that stops short of the kind of explicitness that would get an X, have often opened with antipornography demonstrations going on outside the theater. He isn't hardcore, but he depicts a world in which women are mostly either whores or teases, and their murders are as erotic as their sexual encounters.

In 1984, De Palma blended his customary homage to Alfred Hitchcock's thrillers, his customary stylized simulation of hardcore, and his customary imitation of scenes from his own previous movies for a laugh in *Body Double*. This time, the woman-next-in-line after the cheating wife was a star of the "adult films" business, which has become, in reality, a new legal way for a woman to sell her flesh. As Holly Body, Melanie Griffith sported a white spiked haircut and black lace leotard with a leather miniskirt, when she wore clothes. When the voyeuristic hero, Jake Scully (Craig Wasson) poses as a producer who wants to cast her in order to pump her for information, she feels both obligated and eager to go to bed with him. As a star, however, she has more power to set her own terms than any actress in Harry Cohn, or Darryl Zanuck's stable had. "I get $2000 a day," she tells Jake. "I do not do animal acts. I do not do S & M or any variations of that particular bent. No water sports either. I will not shave my pussy. No fist-fucking, and absolutely no coming in my face." The reason that she must be adamant, of course, is that in adult films the act is real.

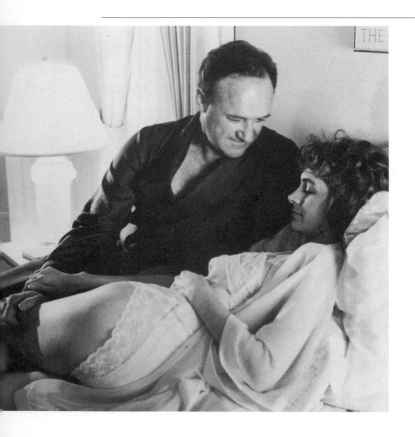

As a little girl, Melanie Griffith saw her mother, Tippi Hedren, lose her chance for a scorching screen career because Alfred Hitchcock adored her and she didn't return the affection. When Griffith was 18, she posed for *Playboy* for $10,000—and now regrets it. Annette Haven, on the other hand, is a real-life star of hardcore who De Palma almost cast as Holly Body. When he auditioned Griffith, he decided that she was a better actress, but he let Haven coach him on the fine points of the hardcore industry, although he ignored her tip that Melanie's hair should not be white and spiky. "Because punk is a neurotic look," she told Susan Dworkin, who wrote a book about De Palma and the making of *Body Double*. "Nobody is going to want to see a punk in an adult movie; not even other punks, I don't think, get off on punks." But he did cut out the dialogue in which Jake asks Holly how she got into the business, and she explains it went back to her penniless childhood in Beauty, Kentucky, where "the only thing to do on a Saturday night was drink beer or slash your wrists." Haven told him that actually she made her first adult film, at 19, for a good time. She was no victim of the economy or anything else, in her mind. "I realized that this would be a very nice position from which to espouse my ideas on sexual education and on sexual health...to make statements to the American public and the world about sexuality," she told Dworkin. Haven reports that she lectures and writes papers, and does stage shows at which she talks about sex, education, and politics.

Nick Broomfield and Sandi Sissel, two filmmakers who went to Nevada in search of a legal whorehouse to film, found that the average noncelebrity flesh-peddler has a tougher lot in life. Long hours, a lecherous boss, money spent as fast as it's earned—the working girls at the real remaining Chicken Ranch dream of getting off the treadmill.

An unsavory man named Walter Plankinton bought a piece of desert land, set

LEFT: *No Way Out*
Sean Young portrays the mistress of Gene Hackman. Ms. Young said: "The strongest feeling I had about her is how polarized she was. She had a kind of warmth and cynicism. She had a super fun time and yet had pain with her all the time." And afterward she said, "She was the most difficult character I've ever had to recover from."

OPPOSITE: *Body Double*
Melanie Griffith asked director Brian De Palma for the part and he replied: "You don't know what you're getting yourself into. Are you sure you want to do it? I think I'm going to use Annette Haven." But he ended up giving Griffith the role, and hiring Haven as her coach. Griffith said, "I believe that some people are judged too readily, and women especially. If you have sex appeal, if you're sexy, it's like the dumb blonde syndrome. Holly is flamboyant and very smart. She's a businesswoman and knows what she's doing."

hero for the yuppie age or an exploiter of other women, Barrows, now 37, told us, "I'm trying to put the whole thing behind me, and I'd appreciate if you wouldn't even mention it in your book." In a movie, that would be the reform scene.

Prim Barrows looked like a schoolgirl next to dazzling Candice Bergen, who played her in the inevitable Hollywoodization of her career, the CBS made-for-TV movie called *The Mayflower Madam*. In the movie, it all starts when Sidney's boyfriend (a script fabrication played by Chris Sarandon) suggests that she start a business of her own. She decides to become a kind of angel of the labor forces, employing the mistreated girls from an escort service run by a slimy pimp. The love interest doesn't see eye to eye with her desire to give women a sense of dignity, and dumps the Mayflower Madam for a mousy little model of propriety played by none other than—Sydney Biddle Barrows.

In her new, albeit short-lived, career as actress and film consultant, Barrows pointed out to reporters that CBS couldn't put the "real story" on the air. Which is? "That it was fun."

In a taste test, however, the knocking shop run by England's notorious madam Cynthia Payne would win hands down for jolly good times, if the contrast between *The Mayflower Madam* and *Personal Services*, starring Julie Walters and directed by the wacky Terry Jones, is an accurate measure. Payne, too, enhanced her fortunes by working as a consultant to the film about "Christine Painter" and her most assuredly kinky specialities and distinguished clientele. Diplomats come to be whipped. A judge—the same judge who presides over the case when Christine is busted—likes to dress in an infinitesimally short skirt and play "lesbian

up a string of trailers, and acquired the name of the original Chicken Ranch in 1970, three years before the best little whorehouse in Texas closed down. To make their documentary, *Chicken Ranch*, Broomfield and Sissel and their crew spent twelve weeks in the trailers, filming the goings-on. "It was kind of like prison. You could never get out of the place," Sissel told us. The girls looked a little burnt out, a little flabby, compared to Dolly Parton's Texas beauties in Hollywood's Chicken Ranch. They must not get much fresh air and exercise during the three weeks of the month that they're on duty, right? It must be hard to preserve your youth in this racket. *Preserve* it? "They're all under 23," said Sissel.

As with most jobs, in the "human fulfillment" trade the wear-and-tear seems to lessen at the top—there is something invigorating about running the company. "Smart cookie," some people said when the world learned that busted "escort service" proprietor Sheila Devin, meticulously groomed in her classic dresses with Puritan-style white collars, was in reality a member of the mainline Biddle clan, descendants of *Mayflower* passengers. Whether she was a folk schoolgirls." Was it Sidney Barrows' Puritan ancestors, who were too straightlaced for in merry old England, that make the difference?

Lizzie Borden, whose docudrama *Working Girls* was released in 1987, the same year as *Mayflower Madam* and *Personal Services*, had a prissy, greedy, vain hussy of a madam looking

OPPOSITE: *Street Smart*
Christopher Reeve portrays a journalist who invents a story about a black pimp. Reeves said he enjoyed doing the research. When the film opened, several dozen Harlem residents picketed, denouncing the stereotyping of blacks as pimps.

BELOW: *Trading Places*
In a switch from the stereotypical view, Eddie Murphy gets vamped by two lovely ladies.

199

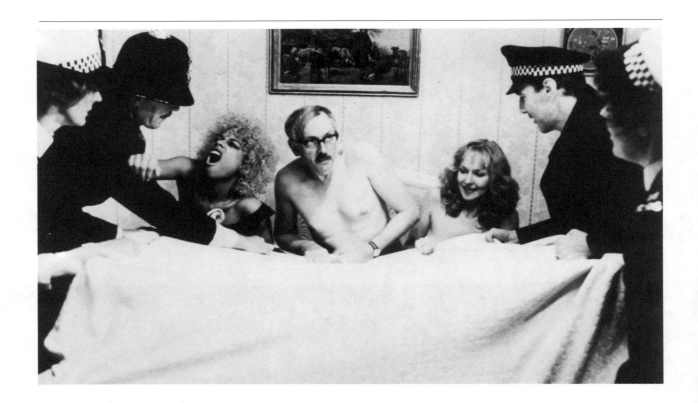

after the brothel "girls" and a generous portion of their earnings. Since Madam Lucy was always quick to point out that she came from a good family, and good schools, the parallels to the Mayflower Madam seemed intentional. "Actually, this was a middle class whorehouse. You'd be amazed at how many of them there are in most major cities, particularly around colleges," said Borden. Sidney Biddle Barrows' establishment was much more exclusive—she charged more than $500 a trick, and the girls had to be perfect, and accomplished, maybe speak five languages."

Three other New York City madams filed suit against Borden after the release of the movie, believing that she had been portraying them.

In researching the movie, Borden found that yuppie prostitutes, of a sort, do exist. "I used to think prostitutes were either street hookers or glamourous high class call girls—extremes," she said. "I was quite amazed to see that there were many women like any

woman you'd see in an office building, or anywhere in middle class society. They were conservative looking, very clean cut, very college....I met a grad student at Columbia who worked at a brothel with a living room that looked like a doctor's waiting room. I met a junior executive at the phone company who quit hooking when she got a promotion."

"I wanted," she said, "to let the viewer be a fly on the wall and see that prostitution isn't really about sex: it's about theatre, it's about manipulation, it's about therapy. You were supposed to see it from the woman's point of view, so that the sex scenes and the woman's body weren't eroticized....One thing that sticks in my mind is that the women who do it for a short time are just fine. Somehow it takes the terror out of dealing with high powered men. Sometimes they emerge wiser, more able to understand men, even see through them instead of being intimidated. But if they stay in it too long it can be a problem. I saw the day girls at Lucy's as being feminist hookers....Gina saving money to buy a boutique, Dawn saving for college, Molly to buy time to be a photographer. Lucy was the *Cosmo* Girl kind of hooker, always thinking about what kind of gifts to get from men."

Working Girls cost $300,000 to make. Borden started with $100,000 in grants, then began seeking investors. "A lot of potential investors," she notes, "said 'I like what you've done so far, but where's the killer?'"

At the turn of the century, the country was engaged in a heated debate over what to do about underaged girls who disappeared from home and became inmates of the red-light quarter. Today the analogous part of town is a strip somewhere, where any passerby can witness much of the action, right on the street. Garish neon will advertise XXX-rated movies for every taste—homo, hetero, and possibly canine or equestrian. Boys, girls, and transvestites will stand on corners, seeking customers. Possibly they are slaves to a pimp, but more likely they are bound by a drug habit, or a lack of any other way to get by, or

OPPOSITE, TOP: *Personal Services*
After a bust like this one, the police often had to release the tricks quickly because they had clout. The real-life madam, Cynthia Payne, said, "Men like sex and women like money." Julie Walters portrayed Madam Payne and met her, saying afterward, "I never actually spoke with her because I couldn't get a word in — and I talk a lot."

OPPOSITE, BOTTOM: *Chicken Ranch*
Sandi Sissel, the woman co-director, was on location when she discussed an unusual incident: "All the girls decided to dress me up to take my place in the line-up. It sort of felt like gang rape. It felt like prison in there, as you were never allowed outside."

ABOVE: *Angel*
The ad read: "An honor student by day, a hooker by night." Angel is being questioned by police about a killer of street girls. Donna Wilkes, the film's star, said: "I'm not a fan of exploitation films." She felt portraying Angel was a good opportunity because, "How many actresses get the chance to play these roles? They're not cutesie parts but meaty roles that require hard work and present a challenge."

both. It is this world that keeps "Angel" self-reliant when both of her parents disappear in the movie of the same name. Donna Wilkes, who played the honor student by day, Hollywood hooker by night, reflected in an interview that a young actress these days can hardly avoid playing a prostitute. "I figure adolescents have so many problems," she said.

"They're runaways. They're addicts, and the media deals with those problems, so that's where a lot of the roles for adolescents are."

In fact, Tiny, one of the runaway kids whose life of hustling on the streets of Seattle was chronicled in *Streetwise*, a 1985 documentary by Martin Bell, Mary Ellen Mark, and Cheryl McCall, is rumored to have received a call from Warren Beatty's office after an endearing photo of her, with a grimy urchin face, blowing a bubble and wearing a retro-fashion veiled pillbox hat, was seen around the world. But she isn't headed for a show-biz career. She's still on the street, reports Bell, and she's lucky—some of the kids shown in the movie are dead now.

There is no fast-track life for child prostitutes. "They come from homes where the pressure is so unbearable that life on the street is more acceptable," says Bell. Shellie, a 13-year-old prostitute when the movie was made, is shown trying to tell her mother that she took to the street because her stepfather had abused her. "Yeah," her mother says, "but he doesn't do it anymore."

Grim reality has made giant strides since the days of the "educational" white slave antivice movies. And the celluloid harlot of Hollywood? She has survived war, sexual revolution, the economy's ups and downs, and emerged with a secure job. She's in an evergreen industry that always keeps its product packaged for the times.

BIBLIOGRAPHY

Addams, Jane. *A New Conscience and an Ancient Evil*. 1912.

Anger, Kenneth. *Hollywood Babylon*. New York: Bell, 1975.

Angly, Edward. Series of three articles on film boycotts. *The Literary Digest*, July 7, 1934; July 14, 1934; July 21, 1934.

Balio, Tino (ed.). *The American Film Industry*. Madison: The University of Wisconsin Press, 1976.

Bell, Martin. Interview with author (J.A.), 1989.

Bodeen, DeWitt. *From Hollywood*. Cranberry, N.J.: A.S. Barnes & Co., 1976.

Borden, Lizzie. Interview with author (J.A.), 1988.

Bowers, Ronald. "Joan Bennett." *Films in Review*, pp. 327 - 337, June - July 1977.

Brown, Peter Harry. *Kim Novak: The Reluctant Goddess*. New York: St. Martin's Press, 1986.

Carey, Gary. *Judy Holliday: An Intimate Life Story*. New York: Seaview Books, 1982.

Cooper, Miriam. *The Dark Lady of the Silents*. New York: Bobbs-Merrill, 1973.

Crist, Judith. "Sex and Violence in Movies and TV: How Harmful Are They?" *Good Housekeeping*, August 1969.

Dandridge, Dorothy, and Conrad, Earl. *Everything and Nothing: The Dorothy Dandridge Tragedy*. New York: Abelard-Schulman, 1970.

Davis, Kingsley. "The Sociology of Prostitution." *ASR*, **2**, pp. 744 - 755, 1937.

Dworkin, Susan. *Double De Palma: A Film Study with Brian De Palma*. New York: Newmarket Press, 1984.

Ehrenreich, Barbara. *The Hearts of Men: American Dreams and the Flight from Commitment*. Garden City, N.Y.: Anchor Books, 1984.

Everson, William K. Interview with author (J.A.), 1982.

Fishbein, Leslie. "Hollywood's Harlots: Prostitution on the Silver Screen, 1900 - 1930." Paper, American Studies Department, Rutgers University, February 1979.

Fishbein, Leslie. Interview with authors, 1982.

Frewin, Leslie. *Dietrich: The Story of a Star*. Rev. ed. London: Publishers Ltd., 1967.

Haden-Guest, Anthony. "The Story of the 'Mayflower Madam'." *New York*, December 10, 1984.

Haskell, Molly. *From Reverence to Rape: The Treatment of Women in the Movies*. New York: Holt, Rinehart and Winston, 1974.

Higham, Charles. *Marlene: The Life of Marlene Dietrich*. New York: W.W. Norton & Co., 1977.

Janus, Samuel. Interview with author (J.A.), 1989.

Kelley, Kitty. *Elizabeth Taylor: The Last Star*. New York: Simon & Schuster, 1981.

Kennedy, Florynce. Interview with authors, 1989.

Kobal, John. *Rita Hayworth: The Time, the Place and the Woman*. London: W.H. Allen, 1977.

Loughney, Patrick. Interview with author (J.A.), 1982.

Lovelace, Linda, with McGrady, Mike: *Out of Bondage*. Secaucus, N.J.: Lyle Stuart, 1986.

Mandelbaum, Howard. Interview with author (J.A.), 1984.

Marion, Frances. *Off with Their Heads*. New York: Macmillan, 1972.

McCarthy, Kathleen D. "Nickel Vice and Virtue: Movie Censorship in Chicago, 1907 - 1915." *Journal of Popular Film*, date unknown.

Moley, Raymond. *The Hays Office*. New York: Bobbs-Merrill, 1945.

Morella, Joe, and Epstein, Edward Z. *The "It" Girl.* New York: Delacorte Press, 1976.

Mosley, Leonard. *Zanuck: The Rise and Fall of Hollywood's Last Tycoon.* Boston: Little, Brown & Co., 1984.

National Dairy Products Corporation. Advertisement (appeared in *Life*, January 6, 1947).

Negri, Pola. *Memoirs of a Star.* New York: Doubleday, 1970.

Nevard, Jacque. "Airline and Union Ponder Issue: Can a Girl Be Too Attractive? *The New York Times*, p. 23, September 27, 1958.

Parish, James Robert. "Theda Bara," in *The Fox Girls.* New York: Castle Books, 1974.

Billy Rose Theatre Collection, New York Public Library at Lincoln Center. Assorted clippings on Theda Bara, Joan Bennett, Ingrid Bergman, Clara Bow, Louise Brooks, Julie Christie, Joan Crawford, Marlene Dietrich, Jane Fonda, Glenn Ford, Greta Garbo, Jean Harlow, Rita Hayworth, Judy Holliday, Shirley MacLaine, Jayne Mansfield, Marilyn Monroe, Alla Nazimova, Pola Negri, Kim Novak, Brooke Shields, Barbara Stanwyck, Anna Sten, Gloria Swanson, Lana Turner, Mae West.

St. John, Adela Rogers. "The Private Life and Loves of Jean Harlow." *Liberty*, pp. 28 - 35, 42 - 43, 52, Summer 1973.

Schumach, Murray. *The Face on the Cutting Room Floor: The Story of Movie and Television Censorship.* New York: William Morrow & Co., 1964.

Sissel, Sandi. Interview with authors, 1983.

Sklar, Robert. *Movie-Made America.* New York: Random House, 1975.

"The Stage" column, *Vanity Fair*, October 1913; November 1913.

Strait, Raymond. *The Tragic Secret Life of Jayne Mansfield.* Chicago: Henry Regnery Co., 1974.

Swanson, Gloria. *Swanson on Swanson.* New York: Random House, 1980.

"Topics of the Day," *Vanity Fair*, March 22, 1913; March 17, 1914.

Tynan, Kenneth. "The Girl in the Black Helmet." *The New Yorker,* June 11, 1979.

Wayne, Jane Ellen. *Crawford's Men.* Englewood Cliffs, N.J.: Prentice-Hall Press, 1988.

Wayne, Jane Ellen. *Stanwyck.* New York: Arbor House, 1985.

West, Mae. *Goodness Had Nothing to Do with It.* Englewood Cliffs, N.J.: Prentice-Hall Press, 1959.

Woloch, Nancy. *Women and the American Experience.* New York: Alfred A. Knopf, 1984.

"Women" column in *Time*, p. 4, March 10, 1923.

Woronov, Mary. Interview with author (J.A.), 1989.

Worthington, George E. "The Night Clubs of New York." *The Survey*, pp. 413 - 417, January 1, 1929.

Zierold, Norman. *Sex Goddesses of the Silent Screen.* Chicago: Henry Regnery, 1973.

INDEX

A directory to the films, actresses, and actors discussed in this volume.

PHOTO CREDITS